CAMBRIDGE LIBRARY COLLECTION

Books of enduring scholarly value

Religion

For centuries, scripture and theology were the focus of prodigious amounts of scholarship and publishing, dominated in the English-speaking world by the work of Protestant Christians. Enlightenment philosophy and science, anthropology, ethnology and the colonial experience all brought new perspectives, lively debates and heated controversies to the study of religion and its role in the world, many of which continue to this day. This series explores the editing and interpretation of religious texts, the history of religious ideas and institutions, and not least the encounter between religion and science.

Evolution and Christianity

Faced with the theories of scientists and philosophers, perhaps most famously Charles Darwin's, late-Victorian theologians were preoccupied with the reconciliation of Christian teaching with their contemporaries' ideas. First published in 1894, this text forms part of a series introducing key areas of Christian theology for the modern audience. Dr James Iverach examines theories of the origins of both the universe and of life within it, finding in intelligence, morality, faith and ethics a unifying and clarifying force that he argues reveals the presence of God's creative process in the history of the universe. Nothing, he claims, occurs by chance, and natural selection simply expresses that the sum total of causes, both internal and external, results in the state in which only the forms of life now observable should exist. This text provides an insight into the late-Victorian philosophy of Christian Darwinism.

T0370672

Cambridge University Press has long been a pioneer in the reissuing of out-of-print titles from its own backlist, producing digital reprints of books that are still sought after by scholars and students but could not be reprinted economically using traditional technology. The Cambridge Library Collection extends this activity to a wider range of books which are still of importance to researchers and professionals, either for the source material they contain, or as landmarks in the history of their academic discipline.

Drawing from the world-renowned collections in the Cambridge University Library, and guided by the advice of experts in each subject area, Cambridge University Press is using state-of-the-art scanning machines in its own Printing House to capture the content of each book selected for inclusion. The files are processed to give a consistently clear, crisp image, and the books finished to the high quality standard for which the Press is recognised around the world. The latest print-on-demand technology ensures that the books will remain available indefinitely, and that orders for single or multiple copies can quickly be supplied.

The Cambridge Library Collection will bring back to life books of enduring scholarly value (including out-of-copyright works originally issued by other publishers) across a wide range of disciplines in the humanities and social sciences and in science and technology.

Evolution and Christianity

JAMES IVERACH

CAMBRIDGE
UNIVERSITY PRESS

CAMBRIDGE UNIVERSITY PRESS

Cambridge, New York, Melbourne, Madrid, Cape Town, Singapore,
São Paolo, Delhi, Dubai, Tokyo

Published in the United States of America by Cambridge University Press, New York

www.cambridge.org
Information on this title: www.cambridge.org/9781108000680

© in this compilation Cambridge University Press 2009

This edition first published 1894
This digitally printed version 2009

ISBN 978-1-108-00068-0 Paperback

THE

THEOLOGICAL EDUCATOR

Edited by the
REV. W. ROBERTSON NICOLL, M.A., LL.D.
Editor of " The Expositor

DR. JAMES IVERACH'S
EVOLUTION AND CHRISTIANITY

London

HODDER AND STOUGHTON

27, PATERNOSTER ROW

MDCCCXCIV

The Theological Educator.

Fcap. 8vo, cloth, price 2s. 6d. each.

EVOLUTION
AND CHRISTIANITY

BY

JAMES IVERACH, M.A., D.D.

PROFESSOR OF APOLOGETICS AND EXEGESIS OF THE GOSPELS IN THE
FREE CHURCH COLLEGE, ABERDEEN

Author of " Is God Knowable ?" "Life of St. Paul," etc.

"Things are also Thoughts, and have a reference to the
Thought that set them there, and to the Thought that finds
them there."

London:

HODDER AND STOUGHTON
27, PATERNOSTER ROW

MDCCCXCIV

CONTENTS

CHAPTER IV.

THE STRIFE AGAINST PURPOSE.

CHAPTER V.

EVOLUTION AND CREATION.

CHAPTER VI.

ORGANIC EVOLUTION.

CHAPTER X.

EVOLUTION AND ETHICS.

CHAPTER XI.

EVOLUTION AND RELIGION.

CHAPTER I

EVOLUTION AND BEGINNINGS

Evolution the working hypothesis of scientific men—Evolution as a dogmatic faith—Truth of evolution—The primitive nebulosity—Spectrum analysis—Star systems—Professor Karl Pearson on lifeless chaotic mass—Chaos unthinkable—Homogeneousness—Evolution must commence somewhere—Its commencement a relative unity.

EVOLUTION is the working hypothesis of most scientific men at the present time. In no branch of science is it without influence, and in the sciences which deal with life it is dominant. We cannot escape from it. Its technical phrases have become parts of current common speech ; and such words as "natural selection," the "struggle for existence," and "the survival of the fittest" are on the lips of every one. It does not matter to what sphere of human work we turn, for in all alike we meet with the same mental atmosphere. Are we students of physics or chemistry, we have no sooner mastered the elements of the science than we are plunged into questions which deal with the "evolution" of the "atom" or the "molecule" from simpler forms of matter. Do we study mechanics, then we are brought into a sphere where men talk of the evolution of the steam engine or of some other

1

machine which has slowly grown from less to more till it has reached its present state. Are we students of man, then we become accustomed to inquiries into the evolution of the family, of marriage, of the community, of the state. Morality is evolved, religion also. On all hands men are busy tracing out the lines of evolution from the general to the particular, from the simple to the complex, until it is affirmed " that the whole world, living and not living, is the result of the mutual interaction, according to definite laws, of the powers possessed by the molecules of which the primitive nebulosity of the universe was composed " (Huxley, *Life of Darwin*, vol. ii., p. 210). It is evident enough that, in these views of Professor Huxley, evolution has passed beyond the stage of a working hypothesis, and has become both a philosophy and a dogmatic faith. We are restricted to molecules, their powers, and the interactions of their powers for the explanation of the universe ; when the molecules are given in their primitive nebulosity, the whole result follows. There can be no increment from without, no guidance from above, nor any leading along a definite line to a predetermined end. The molecules and their interactions must be competent to produce all that has come out in the process. We need not say how great is the issue involved in this claim, nor how strenuously it is to be resisted. It is something gained, however, to have the claims of evolution considered as a dogmatic faith stated so clearly, and to know with what we have to deal.

Manifestly evolution as a working hypothesis and evolution as a dogmatic faith mean very different

things. Even if we grant that it is more than a
working hypothesis—let us grant that it is the highest
scientific generalisation to which the human mind
has yet attained; that in it we have a law of the
widest working which is operative in all the realm
of nature, animate and inanimate—yet this concession
falls far short of the immeasurable demand which
Professor Huxley makes in the name of evolution.
Let us suppose it proved as a scientific generalisation,
and we may still say, with Professor Fraser, " evolution itself, if proved, would be only an expression of
physical causation—of phenomenal significance and
interpretability—though it may yet turn out to be
the most comprehensive of all merely phenomenal laws,
and the highest expression of the sense symbolism, a
physical causation, which Berkeley has so emphatically
contrasted with spiritual and transcendent causality "
(*Fraser on Berkeley*, p. 227). But the advocates of
evolution are not content with the concession that
it is the most comprehensive of all phenomenal laws ;
they demand absolute submission. Evolution must
reign without a rival ; everything must bend to its
sway.

The imperious demands which Professor Huxley,
Mr. Herbert Spencer, and others make in the name
of evolution must not be allowed, however, to
frighten us away from the name, or to blind us to
the truth which is contained in it. Extravagant
claims must not be allowed to discredit legitimate demands. In fact, the real work done by evolution, the
truth set forth by it, the grandeur of its generalisation,
and its consistency with scientific truth generally,

make one sorry when the theory is pushed to an extreme which makes it untrue and inadequate. We are not surprised when the expounders of this theory of the universe are filled with cosmic emotion at the greatness and grandeur of the process they describe; nor do we wonder that they are carried away with the rapture into which they are thrown : for no reader can withhold his sympathy and admiration. It is grand and ennobling to sweep back in thought across the hundred million years or so which separate us from the time when our earth was only vapour, and to be led on from that point of time, through all the intervening ages, as one science after another guides our footsteps, until we arrive at the complex, differentiated, integrated world of the present time, with its life, intelligence, ethics, religion, science, art, and to have some understanding of the process whereby this has come out of that. But we may still have the rapture and the admiration : we may admire and so far revere and be thankful for the work done in the service of evolution, and yet withhold that final sacrifice demanded in her name.

Almost every book on evolution and every magazine article devoted to the subject tries to hark back to the " primitive nebulosity." Not many of them, however, commit themselves to any definite theory on the question of the nebular view. Some, indeed, with a courage which we cannot sufficiently admire, speak as if Kant or Laplace had left nothing for their followers to do. Mr. Fiske is quite sure on the matter. " In the slow concentration of the matter constituting this solar nebula," he says, "as both Kant and

Laplace have elaborately prove l, the most prominent peculiarities of the solar system find their complete explanation " (*Cosmic Philosophy*, vol. i., p. 360). We shall have something to say of this later on. At present we may observe that Professor Huxley's statement does not limit itself to the solar system ; it extends to the universe. The progress of science has made it much more probable that some form of the nebular theory is true. While this is so, any tenable view of the nebular hypothesis, or any view consistent with facts, has presented that hypothesis in a form which is not available for the purposes of evolution. Professor Huxley assumes " a primitive nebulosity of the universe." If this has any meaning, we must try to imagine all the matter of the universe dispersed equally through space, and in a uniform physical condition. If we were to trace the process backwards from the present hour, and try to follow the various steps by which the star systems came to their present condition, we should finally arrive at the primitive nebulosity. But then we should have to explain the fact that there are so many systems that have not yet emerged from their first estate.

Spectrum analysis has made us acquainted with the physical condition of many kinds of stars. If we study such works as Schellen's *Spectrum Analysis*, or Miss Clerke's *System of the Stars*, we shall become acquainted with worlds at all stages of their history. " We can indeed hesitate to admit neither the fundamental identity of the material elements of the universe, nor the nebulous origin of stars. The transition from one to the other of the two great families of the sidereal kingdom is so gradual as to afford a rational conviction that what we see contemporaneously in different objects has been exhibited successively in the same objects. Planetary nebulæ pass into gaseous stars on one side, into nebulous stars on the other, the greater nebulæ into clusters. The present state of the Pleiades refers us inevitably to an antecedent condition closely resembling that of the Orion nebula ; the Andromeda nebula may represent the nascent stage of a splendid collection of suns. But even though stars without exception have sprung from nebulæ, it does not follow that nebulæ without exception grow into stars. The requisite conditions need not invariably have been present. Other ends than that of star production are perhaps subserved by the chief part of the present nebulous contents of the heavens. The contrast between stellar and nebular distribution is intelligible only as expressing a definitive separation of the life-histories of the two classes—a divergence destined to be perpetual along their lines of growth." (*System of the Stars*, p. 396.) Thus we see how naturally astronomy uses the language of evolution, and how the new astronomy with the aid of the mighty instrument of spectrum analysis has added to our knowledge and increased our wonder. A cross section seems to give us also the line of the life-history of a star or a system of stars. And the theory of Kant with regard to the solar system seems to have reference also to the sidereal system. May we by an act of faith go back to the primitive nebulosity of the universe, and, assuming a primitive nebulosity, with known qualities and laws, seek thus to account for the universe? We must start somewhere, and perhaps for some purposes a primitive nebulosity is as good a starting-place as we can have. But we should observe how many things we have assumed, and how much we have taken for granted. We have assumed "molecules possessed of definite powers," that these powers work according to definite laws, and that out of their mutual interaction a definite world of order will arise. Now these are large assumptions, and if granted have raised many important questions. What has been assumed is something definite, and yet the attempt is constantly made to make it indefinite. There is nothing more common than to call the "primitive nebulosity" chaos. "Suppose," says Professor Karl Pearson, "the highly developed reason of some future man to start, say, with clear conceptions of the lifeless chaotic mass of 60,000,000 years ago, which now forms our planetary system, then from these conceptions alone he will be able to *think* out the 60,000,000 years' history of the world with every finite phase which it had passed through; each will have its necessary place, its necessary course in this thought system. And this total history he has thought out? It will be identical with the actual history of the world; for that history has evolved in the sole way conceivable." (*The Ethics of Freethought*, p. 29.)

Apart from the other issues raised by this statement, we concentrate attention on one aspect of it. This we do mainly because Professor Karl Pearson is here a representative writer. Many other people, of less ability than he, speak of a primeval chaos out of which somehow order must emerge. But may we ask how we are to have "clear conceptions of a life-less chaotic mass," whether we consider it as existing a number of years ago or at the present hour? We can only conceive of it just in proportion as we think the chaos away. A mass means something; it has a certain bulk, a certain shape, a certain kind of con-sistency; and if it has these, to speak of it as chaotic is mere rhetoric. A clear conception is possible only if there is something clear to be apprehended; and to speak of a clear conception of a chaos implies something chaotic in the mind which speaks.

The primitive nebulosity, if it ever existed, was as definite, as much subject to law, as clearly marked by definite qualities, as the universe which is supposed to have evolved out of it. At all events, it existed in a definite material state; it occupied space; molecules or atoms, or the material which afterwards aggregated into atoms or molecules, were there. There were definite laws at work, and there were mutual inter-actions; and just in proportion as these existed, clear conceptions of the so-called "lifeless chaotic" mass are or were possible.

If the primitive nebulosity had any qualities what-soever, then all the advantages which were gained by calling it chaotic are lost. Somehow, I do not know how, but there seems to be a hazy idea in the minds of many, that if a start can be made in chaos, and afterwards a cosmos appears, a solution of the problem of creation has been obtained. Given a

chaotic primitive nebulosity, and given clear conceptions of it, then the universe must arise : such is the
problem and its solution.   But we have no account of
the transition, nor any rational attempt to show why
and how chaos should cease and cosmos begin.   This
difficulty besets the mechanical theory of the universe
as it besets every other theory.   How to get our
starting-point is the perplexity.   We cannot begin
with chaos; and if we begin with anything definite,
where have we got it ?   We may place the elephant
on the back of the tortoise, but what will support the
tortoise ?

It is amazing that those who assume the primitive
nebulosity ˙do not see that it raises precisely those
questions concerning order, its source, method, and
law, which are raised by the universe as at present
constituted.   It raises these questions also in a form
more difficult of solution.   We may not ask how
this nebulous mass came to be; if we did ask, we
should at once be told that we must not inquire
regarding origins.   Leaving origins, then, we may
ask whether the mass is constituted so and so, and in
such a manner as to make a certain result inevitable.
If, as Professor Karl Pearson says, "the universe
is what it is because *that* is the only conceivable
fashion in which it could be—in which it could be
thought "—we may conclude that thought has gone
to the making of it.   If thought has come out of the
universe, if the universe is a universe which can be
thought, then thought has had something to do with
it from the outset.   There is thought in the primitive
nebulosity, and thought of the most marvellous kind.

But we can scarcely ascribe the thought to the molecules, Whence has it come? We humbly submit that at this stage we require more thought to make clear what we mean.

If instead of Professor Karl Pearson's chaotic mass we take the indefinite, incoherent homogeneity of Mr. Herbert Spencer, we have not made any advance. Suppose we grant the possibility of such a homo—geneity, we cannot get it to act. Mr. Spencer himself recognises this: "One stable homogeneity only is hypothetically possible. If centres of force, absolutely uniform in their powers, were diffused with absolute uniformity through unlimited space, they would remain in equilibrium. This, however, though a verbally intelligible supposition, is one which cannot be repre-sented in thought, since unlimited space is inconceivable. But all finite forms of the homogeneous, all forms of it which we can know or conceive, must inevitably lapse into heterogeneity." (*First Principles*, p. 429.) The homogeneity which his system demands is dismissed as inconceivable, "since unlimited space is inconceivable." And then he proceeds to speak of "all finite forms of the homogeneous"; and by so doing cuts down the only branch on which he can sit. A finite form of the homogeneous is really destructive of his hypothesis. For the finiteness of the form postulates a difference between the homo-geneous and its environment; and as that difference is both continuous and active, it will not allow the homogeneous to exist. The very notion of a finite homogeneity is self-destructive.

Another result follows. The objection which is

brought against absolute homogeneity implies that the absolute or the ultimate reality can manifest itself only in finite forms. Any other than a finite manifestation, "though a verbally intelligible proposition, is one that cannot be represented in thought, since the unlimited is inconceivable." How contradictory this is of many of Mr. Spencer's propositions we need not here determine. But the remark that "unlimited space is inconceivable" does not hinder him from saying on the same page, "The absolutely homogeneous must lose its equilibrium," and yet "they would remain in equilibrium." Hence we have this dilemma : If the homogeneous is absolute, it will remain in equilibrium ; if the equilibrium is disturbed, then the homogeneity is not absolute.

How does evolution commence according to Mr. Spencer ? "All finite powers of the homogeneous— all forms of it which we can know or conceive—must inevitably lapse into heterogeneity. In three several ways does the persistence of force necessitate this. Setting external agencies aside, each unit of a homogeneous whole must be differently affected from any of the rest by the action of the rest on it. The resultant force exercised by the aggregate on each unit, being in no two cases alike in both amount and direction, and usually not in either, any incident force, even if uniform in amount and direction, cannot produce like effects on the units. And the various positions of the parts in relation to any incident force preventing them from receiving them in uniform amounts and directions, a further difference in the effects wrought on them is inevitably produced."

(*First Principles*, p. 429.)   Let any one try to think out these propositions.   " Each unit of a homogeneous whole must be differently affected from any of the rest by the aggregate action of the rest on it."   Why ?   The necessity is not apparent.   If a whole be homogeneous, then it would result that each unit must be similarly affected by the aggregate action of the rest on it.   If it be differently affected, whence the difference ?   If the difference be one in position, then homogeneity has vanished and heterogeneity has begun.   Every attempt made by Mr. Spencer to make a commencement postulates difference, and any difference is destructive of the homogeneity.   At the beginning of all evolution he has to bring in somehow actual differences, real adjustments, and relations, and yet he endeavours to evolve these out of an original simplicity.   Evolution has to begin, not from a minimum simplicity, but from what looks like a rational, intelligible adjustment of means to ends, and of qualities and properties in relation ; and this is exactly the theistic position.

The primitive nebulosity of Professor Huxley, the lifeless chaotic mass of Professor Karl Pearson, the absolutely homogeneous of Mr. Spencer, and, we may add, similar postulates of other writers, do not serve the purpose of those who have introduced them to our notice.   They do not help us to pass from the indeterminate to the determinate, and they do not help us to get intelligence out of what is not intelligent.   Every problem presented by the present complex universe is presented also by the primitive nebulosity.   It is an attempt to get what is adjusted out of what is not adjusted, relations out of what has none, and differences out of that which has no difference. Every step proceeds on what has been formally denied, and the result is mere confusion of thought ; for evolution can commence only when change begins, and the absolutely homogeneous, if left to itself, cannot even begin to change. Thus we are at the outset constrained to postulate some force outside of the homogeneous in order that change may begin ; or if the beginning of change is due to something within the homogeneous, then we have difference to start with. There is no way of escape from the thought of prearranged activities within the mass which Professor Karl Pearson calls chaotic.

Prearranged activities, however, is the very supposition of which the writers in question seek to get rid. They value the primitive nebulosity just in proportion as it enables them to make a beginning, and to get the work of intelligence without the help of intelligence. It is just the old attempt of trying to get something out of nothing. We are not to ask any question about the primitive nebulosity. We are not to ask how it happened to be there, nor inquire into its previous history, if it had a history. We are to be willing to take it for granted. At a certain time, many millions of years ago, there existed a primitive nebulosity, an undifferentiated chaotic mass of matter, in an extremely attenuated form, equally balanced in all directions, and each part of it indistinguishable from every other part. It is homogeneous throughout. Let us suppose also that the mass is in what may be called the pre-chemical state of matter.

What is now known as atoms and molecules has not yet come to be. The different chemical elements have not yet aggregated together. There is one stuff, and only one, and each part of it is identical with every other part. Let us grant the supposition. It is possible that such stuff has existed. The experiments and reasonings of Mr. Norman Lockyer have made it at least possible. The chemical elements may be various combinations of one uniform stuff. There may have been a time when matter was absolutely homogeneous. But the supposition does not help us. For somehow change has to begin and change has to continue, and has to continue in one direction. As soon as change has begun the undifferentiated stuff becomes differentiated, the indeterminate becomes determinate, and the chemical elements appear. When once they are made they are never unmade. It is not necessary for our purpose to inquire as to whether science can trace the genesis of the molecule; for all the kinds of matter we know are gathered up into various limited sorts, and each of these sorts is practically indestructible. " Though in the course of ages catastrophes have occurred and may yet occur in the heavens, though ancient systems be dissolved and new systems evolved out of their ruins, the molecules out of which these systems are built, the foundation-stones of the material universe, remain unbroken and unworn." So speaks Professor Clerk Maxwell. Again he says: " There are immense numbers of atoms of the same kind, and the constituents of each of these atoms are incapable of adjustment by any powers now in action. Each is physically independent of all the others. Whether or not the conception of a multitude of beings existing from all eternity is in itself self-contradictory, the conception becomes palpably absurd when we attribute a relation of quantitative equality to all these beings. We are then forced to look beyond them to some common cause or common origin to explain why this singular relation of equality exists, rather than any of the infinite number of possible relations of inequality. Science is incompetent to reason on the creation of the world out of nothing. We have reached the utmost limit of our thinking faculties when we have admitted that, because matter cannot be eternal and self-existent, it must have been created." (*Encyc. Brit.*, vol. iii., art. " Atom," p. 49, 9th ed.) We should like to ask whether the primitive nebulosity is composed of definite atoms and molecules or not. If it is in the pre-atomic stage pictured by Mr. Norman Lockyer, then clearly its first work is to become atomic. If it has become atomic, then we have no longer to deal with a homogeneous kind of stuff, but with a stuff that has got itself packed into sixty or seventy different kinds—kinds which persist, which no power can change, and no use can wear out. The problem thus becomes infinitely more complicated. It is not now a case of the absolutely homogeneous losing its equilibrium, and thus in-stituting a series of changes; but it becomes a problem of how to obtain a unity out of sixty or seventy different sets of things, each set of which is different from all the others, and of each set there is an incalculable number. The problem is not how to obtain otherness out of unity, but to gather the differences into a unity. An abstract unity will not suffice. It is not enough to abstract from the difference of each separate set of molecules, and generalise them all under the common name of matter; nor to abstract from the various energies at work in the universe, and generalise them under the common name of force : what is needed is a kind of unity which shall keep the differences, and recognise the special nature of each kind. And this is a unity made up of relations. Thus at the very basis of the material system there is evidence of rationality of the very highest order. Given sixty or seventy different kinds of stuff, each with its own proper qualities and attributes, to make out of them a stable and progressive universe—that is the problem; and it is one evidently of a higher kind than that presented to us by Mr. Spencer.

Thus we have the theistic problem and answer before evolution can be said to have begun. Whether these molecules have had a previous history or not, at all events they have passed now out of any sphere which can be influenced by the struggle for existence. A molecule of hydrogen continues to be a molecule of hydrogen wheresoever it may be, in whatsoever combination it may exist, and whatsoever work it may be doing. If it ever had to struggle for existence, it has long ago got past that stage. It exists, it cannot be changed, it does work, and about it evolution has nothing to say. And yet the problem of its existence and its qualities and its relations is as great as those which evolution is called on to solve.

CHAPTER II

EVOLUTION AND LAW

Nature is what is fixed, stated, settled—Law and hypothesis —The nebular theory—Its plausibilities and its difficulties—The nebular theory and evolution—It involves a rational system—The theistic argument—Continuity— Evolution a real process—" Instability of the homogeneous "—Multiplication of effects—" Is the effect more complex than the cause ? "—Criticism of this statement.

THE unity of the primitive nebulosity must have been, as we have seen, a unity of elements in relation to one another. It is not undifferentiated stuff, but definite molecules existing in definite relations. It is not chaotic, but orderly, and existing in relations which can be thought. Thus the unity of the primitive nebulosity is already rational and intelligible. If this is possible at the outset, then the process of evolution will also be rational and intelligible, ànd the outcome will also be rational. It is not for us to contend against the existence of a primitive nebulosity either of the solar system or of the sidereal. Nor have we any interest in contending against the discovery of method, order, law in nature. We are glad to sit at the feet of those who can show us the widening bounds of order and law, who can teach us to know the dominion of order and law

where we were once unable to discover it.   We gladly
follow Mr. Herbert Spencer as he leads us on from
stage to stage of existence and of knowledge, and
shows us how every stage is under law, and that even
the very discovery of law is itself subject to law.
We may not agree with him either in the general or
in the particular, but we are grateful for the wide
outlook he has cast over the universe, and for a
possible interpretation of the order of nature.   We
had learned from Bishop Butler that the meaning
of nature is what is fixed, settled, determined, and
that what is fixed and settled has had reference to
some cause which made it so.

Thus we were prepared in the interests of theology
to welcome every conquest of science and every fresh
proof of the universal reign of law.   The Bishop
had taught us to look for the traces of the Divine
footsteps, not in what appears to be lawless and
capricious and arbitrary, but in that which was
fixed, steadfast, determined.   Thus, on the principles
of Bishop Butler,—which are also the principles of
a true theology,—we are to wait for the instructions
of our masters in science.   They are the true inter-
preters of nature, as they are also the discoverers of
its laws.   They have proved that the law according
to which a stone falls to the ground is the law
according to which the planets describe their orbits
and the stars maintain their places.   And if they
tell us that the earliest known form of the solar
system is that of a gaseous nebula, and if they can
prove this to be the fact—well, then we accept the
fact, and act accordingly.   If they tell us that the

widest law known to them is that of evolution, that by the way of evolution the universe has come to be what it is—well, if it is so, we see no more reason why we should be disturbed by evolution than we have been by gravitation. Neither gravitation nor evolution is ultimate, and when science has done its work something remains to be said.

Let us therefore without hesitation follow our scientific teachers, with the sure belief that they do us service whenever they can disclose to us order and method and law in nature. They also will no doubt tell us what has been proven and what is only probable. They will observe, we hope, this distinction, and will give us due notice when they leave the firm ground of proof and take to speculation. And we have a right to expect that they will keep hypothesis separate from ascertained law. For the most part, we have no reason to complain. We get sublime speculation, but we also get profound calculation; and as a rule these are kept separate. With reference to the matter before us, the primitive nebulosity and the nebular theory, for the most part competent men deal with it as a speculation, and not as a certainty. Laplace himself did so. He placed the nebular hypothesis on a different footing from his statement about the stability of the solar system. This was a proof that all the changes of the solar system were periodic, that if it is disturbed a little it will oscillate and return to its old state. This demonstration proceeded on the assumption that the planets were rigid bodies, and on that assumption the demonstration is complete. Corrections have to be made because the planets are not rigid bodies; but these do not concern us here. The point is that Laplace himself threw out his suggestion of the nebular theory simply as a speculation. The theory of the stability of the solar system followed with inevitable certainty from the theory of gravitation. But the nebular theory could not be deduced from the theory of gravitation, and must continue to rank only as a hypothesis. It has its difficulties, and it has its probabilities; but as yet science does not affirm its truth.

Its probabilities are, to use the language of Sir Robert S. Ball : " Many of the features in the solar system harmonise with the supposition that the origin of the system has been that suggested by the nebular theory. We have already had occasion in an earlier chapter to allude to the fact that all the planets perform their revolution around the sun in the same direction. It is also to be observed that the rotation of the planets on their axes, as well as the movements of the satellites around their primaries, are following the same law, with one slight exception in the case of the Uranian system. A coincidence so remarkable naturally suggests the necessity for some physical explanation. Such an explanation is offered by the nebular theory. Suppose that countless ages ago a mighty nebula was slowly rotating and slowly contracting. In the process of contracting portions of the condensed matter would be left behind. These portions would still revolve round the central mass, and each portion would rotate on its axis in the same direction. As the process of contraction proceeded it would follow from dynamical principles that the velocity of rotation would increase ; and thus at length these portions would consolidate into masses, while the central mass would gradually contract to form the sun. By a similar process on a smaller scale the systems of satellites were evolved from the contracting primary. These satellites would also revolve in the same direction, and thus the characteristic features of the solar system could be accounted for." (*Story of the Heavens*, p. 501.) The language is exceedingly cautious. It is said " many of the features in the solar system harmonise with the supposition." " Thus the features of the solar system could be accounted for." Sir Robert Ball does not say, " They are accounted for." This is very different from the statement already quoted about the primitive nebulosity, and very different from what is required by the part which the nebular theory is made to play in the theory of evolution. What was the state of the nebula ? Was it hot or cold ? We must think of the matter of it as in some state. Are we to think of the matter of the nebula as consisting of the same kinds of atoms as those we know to-day ? Were these atoms arranged according to their specific gravities ? If they were, the heaviest would gravitate to the centre and the lighter would gather at the circumference ; but the whole business must somehow arrange itself so that the earth, for example, may start fair and have capital enough for all its expenditure. A nebula abandoned to the influence of gravity, and left to shape itself as it might, is yet to be so conceived as to provide a suitable endowment for each member of the family. It looks at this stage as if the nebular hypothesis needed to be supplemented.

" Suppose that countless ages ago a mighty' nebula was slowly rotating and slowly contracting." It is easy to make the supposition, and yet exceedingly difficult to realise what is involved in it. The matter of the nebula is exceedingly rare, so attenuated that the matter of the solar system stretched beyond the bounds of the orbit of the most distant planet. Mr. Proctor declares that in such a system rotation is impossible; and it is indeed difficult to conceive a continuous rotation of such an attenuated body.

It is an essential part of the theory, in the use made of it by evolution, that no help can be brought to the nebula from without. It is a self-contained system, and all its energy is contained within itself, and its quantity of energy cannot be increased or diminished. Unless, however, we postulate action of a force beyond the system, it is difficult to see how there should be any rings cast off from the whirling mass. As the mass contracts the gravitation increases, and at the same time the rate of rotation grows more rapid. The possibility of forming a ring, or of detaching it from the main body, depends on the relation between the centripetal and centrifugal forces. The application of the theory to the present solar system depends on the ability of the theory to demonstrate that at the various orbits of the planets the centrifugal forces increased by precisely so much as to necessitate the breaking off of just such masses and no more as make up the various planets from Neptune to Mercury. Again, the theory would seem to require that the orbits of the planets would bear some relation to the orbit traced by the equator of the central body where each particular planet has broken off. But there is really no relation between the two.

The nebular hypothesis has as yet afforded no explanation of the distribution of matter throughout the solar system, nor of the size of the planets, nor of their relative density; as a mechanical explanation it has so far failed, and if we are to have an explanation of the solar system, we shall need something more than can be given us by the primitive nebulosity. " A mighty nebula slowly rotating and slowly contracting" does not explain much. It will not explain, for instance, the number of chemical elements in the earth. Take, for example, what we know of the constitution of the nebula in Orion. " We see that it consists in part of stars, making up perhaps in number for their deficiency in size. These stars are bathed in and surrounded by a stupendous mass of glowing gas, partly consisting of that gas which enters so largely into the composition of our ocean, namely, hydrogen. The wide distribution of this substance, the lightest of all the known elements, is one of the most striking facts in the material constitution of the universe." (*Story of the Heavens*, p. 462.) May not the reason why hydrogen is so conspicuous in the spectrum of the nebula in Orion simply be because it is the lightest of all the known elements, and is thus farthest removed from the centre of attraction? Might we not expect, then, that the farthest distant of the planets would also be the lightest? But the density of Saturn is less than the density of Uranus, and the density of Venus is less than that of the Earth. Be that as it may, our present contention is, that the nebular hypothesis is not of a kind to bear the weight laid on it by the theory of universal evolution.

The nebular hypothesis is a very fascinating one, and we need not be surprised that in the hands of Mr. Fiske, for example, it is made to do large service to his cosmic philosophy. Nor are we concerned to deny whatsoever truth may be in it. We know that there are nebulæ in the universe, and that, for example, the great nebula in Andromeda " is in a state of extensive and majestic whirl"; we may also have some conception of the relative distribution of stars and nebulæ : but as for a theory of the life-history of a star or of a system of stars, science at present has none. Our astronomy is so advanced just because we know so little about the planets or the stars. That is to say, we have had to do with planets in the mass, and have dealt only with their masses, orbits, rotation, and other matters of the same sort. But such mechanical knowledge is altogether insufficient for the purpose for which it is sometimes used. That purpose is mainly to show that the mechanism of the heavens is self-explanatory. The solar system is so far self-explanatory, if we are allowed to postulate the stability of the system as an end in view, and the various positions, sizes, and relations of the planets as subservient to that end. Apart from that end the various adjustments are unintelligible and incalculable.

The nebular theory does not explain even the mechanics of the system, far less does it explain the life-history of it. By its vague and general terms, and its wide and grand sweep, it has seemed to accomplish much, and it falls in so well with the general tendency, that we are not surprised to find it bulk so largely in current literature. It advances from the simple to the complex in so charming a way, it seems to assume so little and accomplish so much, that people are quite delighted with it. But when the theory is adjusted to the facts, its simplicity is gone, and what it has accomplished is not so great after all. Thus, with regard to the nebular theory, we are brought back to a position similar to that which confronted us before. The unity we have to start with is not simple, but complex. It is again a unity of related elements, and thus a unity which is not merely material; it is also rational. It is not as if we could get a simplicity to which we may add complexities, or out of which we could evolve complexities, but something different. If we have a naked simplicity, it will not work. But the primitive nebulosity has many elements in it. It has at least matter in a certain state; what that state is we cannot well say. It has a certain rotation, slow it may be, but with a certain momentum, which must be equal to the sum of all the separate momenta existing in the solar system at the present hour. It has a certain bent and direction, and the union of these elements and tendencies has to be accounted for. As with the elements of matter, so with the solar system, the unity we have to start with is an ideal, a rational unity, and the mere mechanics of the system gives no rational explanation of the system.

The interest we have in the primitive nebulosity is

simply a scientific one.   For the purpose of our argument it would make no difference if the theory were
as complete as the theory of the tides.   Every one
knows, more or less, what has been done by Professor
G. H. Darwin with regard to the theory of the tides.
It is not our purpose to describe his theory of tidal
evolution, nor to sketch the history of investigation
with regard to the tides from the time of Newton
onwards.   It is a fascinating story ; but the point in
view at present is this, that when you have completed
the mechanical theory of anything the explanation
is not ultimate.   We are not of those who are constantly looking about for imperfections in a mechanical or other theory in order to find a chink through
which the theistic argument may enter.   Such a
process would be a hopeless task.   If that were our
position, the argument for theism would soon be a
fugitive and vagabond on the face of the earth ; each
advance of science, each discovery of law would simply
drive the theistic argument to seek a new refuge.   On
the contrary, our position is that each new discovery is
a fresh testimony to theism, and each new law found
in phenomena is only a fresh argument for God,—for
intelligence as the source of order and the only ground
of law.   Our argument so far has been to the effect
that the simplicity assumed by evolutionists as the
starting-point of evolution will not work.   What is
required, even on their own theory, is the simplicity
of many elements in a related whole, and such a
unity is rational.

It is to be remembered also that the task of evolution is to deal with the process of evolution as a real

process, to describe real changes which take place, or
have taken place, or will take place in a real world.
There are some sciences in which no error need be
introduced by our beginning with abstractions. It
does no harm in geometry to assume points which
have position and not magnitude, lines which have
length and no breadth, and other abstractions which
have no place in a concrete world ; for in applying
our mathematical deductions to a real world we make
allowances and supply the additional concrete conditions which our abstractions formerly neglected. Nor
does it entail any serious consequences when in
mechanics we assume a perfectly rigid body, a perfectly
rigid lever, a perfect gas, or any other assumption of
the same kind ; for we know all the time that there
are no such bodies to be found. If we were compelled
to take account of every movement of a crowbar, no
calculus at our command is sufficient for the purpose.
We recognise that our physical and dynamical theories
are only of limited application, and we do not try to
deduce the phenomena of a real world from them.
We recognise that, though the orbits of the planets ap-
proximate to an ellipse, there are many perturbations.
For the sake of simplicity in our mathematical and
mechanical science we neglect many elements, but
when we apply our science to actual concrete conditions we have to bring back the elements we formerly
neglected. In physics we neglect chemical conditions,
and in chemistry we neglect vital conditions ; but no
problem is merely physical or mathematical. But
for a complete explanation we have to take all conditions into account.

But this method is one which the evolutionist may not use. He has a larger work than that of the physicist, or the chemist, or the physiologist, or that of the worker in any special department. He has undertaken to explain everything, and to show how change began, and how change went on from stage to stage, necessarily and inevitably. From one stage to another the process must be such as to admit of no alternative. Chance must be eliminated, and the result must be necessary. It will not do to use the method which has been found so useful in mathematics and physics. For we do not try to deduce the properties of matter from mathematical laws. From the law of gravitation we do not try to deduce the particular states of the matter under gravitation. It may be solid, liquid, gaseous; but in whatever state it may be, it is under the law which prescribes that the attraction varies directly as the masses and inversely as the square of the distance. But from this law we can infer nothing as to the state of matter in any place or at any time. It is different, however, with evolution. It can neglect nothing, leave nothing out of account; for it has to explain everything. Its primitive nebulosity must be more strictly defined, its absolute homogeneity must have some other attributes in addition to that absolute sameness if changes are to flow from it. As described by the leading advocates of evolution, the condition of things from which they start is simply an abstraction, to be compared with the points of geometry and the rigid bodies of mechanics. These no doubt are useful things in their way, but their usefulness has only a limited scope.

Similarly the persistence of force is a barren notion until it is transformed into the particular energies of the concrete world in which we live. The difficulty is to make the transition, and certainly Mr. Herbert Spencer has not made it. He labours as in the very fire to bring his abstraction into relation with the concrete world. He cannot deduce differences without assuming the differences he seeks to deduce. His law of the "Instability of the Homogeneous" is self-contradictory; for the two terms of the so-called conception will not unite. If the homogeneous is homogeneous it is stable, and if it is unstable it is not homogeneous. Also when we read his chapter on the "Multiplication of Effects," we see it might as well have the name of the multiplication of causes. "When a uniform aggregate is subject to a uniform force we have seen that its constituents, being differently conditioned, are differently modified. But while we have contemplated the various parts of the aggregate as thus undergoing unlike changes, we have not yet contemplated the unlike changes simultaneously produced on the various parts of the incident force. These must be as numerous and important as the others. Action and reaction being equal and opposite, it follows that in differentiating the parts on which it falls in unlike ways the incidental force must itself be correspondingly differentiated. Instead of being as before a uniform force, it must thereafter be a multiform force—a group of dissimilar forces." (*First Principles*, p. 431.)

Mr. Spencer proceeds to illustrate his principle. We take one of his illustrations: "When one body is struck against another, that which we usually regard as the effect is a change of position or motion in one or both bodies. But a moment's thought shows that this is a very incomplete view of the matter. Beside the visible mechanical result sound is produced; or, to speak accurately, a vibration in one or more bodies, and in the surrounding air. Moreover, the air has not simply been made to vibrate, but has had currents raised in it by the transit of the bodies. Further, if there is not that great structural change which we call fracture, there is a disarrangement of the particles of the two bodies around their point of collision; amounting in some cases to a visible condensation. Yet more, this condensation is accompanied by disengagement of heat. In some cases a spark—that is, light—results from the incandescence of a portion struck off; and consequently this incandescence is associated with chemical combination. Thus by the original mechanical force expended in the collision, at least five, and often more, different kinds of forces have been produced" (pp. 432, 433). Out of one original uniform force we seem to get a multitude of effects, and the law of the multiplication of effects seems established.

Is it really so? Can all these effects be considered as the result of one cause? It is Mr. Spencer's manner to try to get first a simplicity, and then to get a complexity out of it. What is the simplicity here? He has first assumed two bodies and a collision between them. Then he fixes our thought on the bare collision, and will allow us to think of nothing else. But the collision cannot be considered alone in such a case. It is a problem of two bodies, not of a single uniform force. Then he assumes the constitution of the atmosphere ; other assumptions follow, with their results. The changes he describes are not and cannot be truly described as the result of one force. They are the resultant of many forces; and the action of each of them has to be taken into account in order to explain the resultant. He first makes an artificial abstraction of the force expended in the collision, and then tries to trace out its effects. The fact is, that each effect described is simply the combination of the one uniform force assumed, and the other forces he has left out of sight.

"Universally, then, the effect is more complex than the cause." Thus he states his conclusion—a very useful conclusion for his purpose, but one which does not seem to have a logical justification. It does not seem to consist with the law of causation. An adequate cause is one which can completely account for the effect. One of the gravest charges which Mr. Spencer brings against certain thinkers is that they have not a due regard to causation. But what of himself ? If the effect is more complex than the cause, whence has the complexity come ? Can we account for it ? Certainly the illustrations drawn from a collision and from a lighted candle do not justify his universal law. The complexity is only apparent. For in order to produce the complexity he is compelled to set forth the collision as taking place in a complex of relations, and it is through these relations alone that the complexity is made possible. With regard to the lighted candle, he is compelled to place it in the midst of various surroundings, and the process of burning is in relation with each of these. Take away the surroundings, and the changes cannot take place. But surely, in any possible view of a cause, we must take into account all the conditions necessary for the production of the effect. If we take these into account, we shall be constrained to say the cause is as complex as the effect. It is not logical first to place the cause in isolated abstraction, and to set the effect in concrete relations, and on the basis of this illogical procedure gravely to set forth a universal law to the effect that universally the effect is more complex than the cause.

It is well to call attention to this so-called law, for it meets us everywhere in the course of the argument for evolution. It lies at the basis of Mr. Spencer's view of the persistence of force. It gives strength, the only strength it has, to the curious statements about the primitive nebulosity so widely current nowadays. It meets us in chemistry; it is present in biology; it is current in the application of evolution to psychology, ethics, and religion. It is well to face it frankly, and to estimate its value. For it seems to me to be an attempt to get something out of nothing, and in essence to be equivalent to the crudest notion of creation ever present in the minds of men. The cause of evolution must be at least as complex as the result which has emerged. The principles of cosmical multiplicity must lie in the power from which all things have proceeded.

CHAPTER III

NATURE AND INTELLIGIBILITY

Additional factors—Transition from physics to chemistry—
Chemical elements—Their character, relations, adapta-
tions, periodicity—Rational character of these relations—
Nature is intelligible, and therefore related to intelligence
—Attempts at explanation—The chemical elements exist
in the unity of one system.

THE maxim that the effect is more complex than
the cause may be briefly described as the method
of Mr. Spencer. At all the transition stages of his
great system it has impelled him to search for a new
starting period of sufficient simplicity out of which he
can evolve a complex effect. When he begins to deal
with biology, it leads him to accept the structureless
homogeneous cell as the beginning of organic life,
and out of it he obtains all the complexities of
animated being. The unit of consciousness consists
or begins with a sudden nerve shock. "Mind is
certainly in some cases, and probably in all, re-
solvable into nervous shocks" (*Psychology*, i., sect. 62);
and out of a simple nerve shock he tries to build up
mind. The primal simplicity of the phenomena of
religion he finds in ancestor worship. He has a way,
too, of manufacturing intuitions as he needs them.
We come to expect, as we turn from one of his treatises

3

to another, that at the opening of each we shall find a simple cause and a number of complex effects. We anticipate what is coming. The only surprise that awaits us is the precise kind of simplicity which Mr. Spencer will postulate. Some kind he is sure to have, but whether it is an available kind is another question.

We may have to look at some of those simplicities of his further on. Meanwhile let us try his method at an early stage. How does his homogeneous stand related to the chemical elements? We learn from Clerk Maxwell that these chemical elements are indestructible, and cannot be made to decay. They are as they were. We can call them all by the name of matter, because they have properties in common; but each one of them has its own peculiarities, and also its peculiar relation to all the others. Dealing with the classification of the sciences, Mr. Spencer speaks thus : " Theoretically all the concrete sciences are adjoining tracts of one science, which has for its subject-matter the continuous transformation which the universe undergoes. Practically, however, they are distinguishable as successively more specialised parts of the total science—parts further specialised by the introduction of additional factors " (*Psychology*, vol. i., p. 137). " The new factor which differentiates chemistry from molecular physics is the heterogeneity of the molecules with whose redistributions it deals " (p. 140). The description may be accepted as so far true as regards the distinctions between these two sciences. But does Mr. Spencer also make a distinction in nature corresponding to the distinction between physics and chemistry? " Physics," he tells us truly, " deals with changes in the distribution of matter and motion considered apart from unlikeness of quality in the matter." But this may be interpreted in two ways. It may mean that we neglect or do not take into account any unlikeness of quality in the matter, while all the time we know that the unlikeness is there. It may also mean that we deny any unlikeness of quality, and proceed as if it were altogether uniform. We have not been able to gather from Mr. Spencer's writings which of these is meant by him. Sometimes he seems to mean the one, sometimes the other. From his doctrine of homogeneity he seems to postulate a matter without any unlikeness of quality, in which unlikeness would by-and-by appear. That is, however, an assumption which has not yet been proved, which chemists say has been disproved. " We might perhaps be inclined to conceive a chemical process in the following manner : substances consist of indifferent matter, which during any chemical process simply becomes invested with different properties from those which it originally possessed, without, however, itself undergoing any real alteration. This conception was, as a matter of fact, for a long time prevalent ; but the following laws empirically discovered are in discordance with it : if one substance is transformed into another, then the masses of these two substances always bear a fixed ratio to each other ; such a transformation of one substance into another of different mass can only take place according to the first law when a second substance participates in the reaction. The following law, therefore, is in intimate connection with that given above : if several substances react together, then these masses, as well as those of the new bodies formed, always bear fixed proportions to each other." (*Outlines of General Chemistry*, by Wilhelm Ostwald, English translation, p. 4.) Physics knows, however, that it has to deal with elements of unlike qualities, though it lays stress mainly on qualities which they have in common. It knows that within limits all gases obey Boyle's law, and curves have been constructed showing the paths of deviation from that law taken by each particular gas. It recognises also, according to Avogadro's law, that "in equal volumes of different gases there is under the same conditions the same number of molecules." It recognises also different substances, and endeavours to register the different temperatures at which each particular body passes from the gaseous into the liquid state. But on the whole, and generally, physics abstracts from the particular unlikenesses of quality between the different bodies, and leaves that to be dealt with by its own particular science. But the distinction between the sciences is simply a matter of convenience. It does not represent a division in the nature of things.

The new factor in chemistry is simply that factor which physics found it convenient to neglect; but each atom of matter dealt with in physics had also its chemical characters and relations. We find, indeed, that Mr. Spencer did make an attempt to deal with the question from this point of view. In the first edition of the *First Principles* there was a chapter on " The Conditions Essential to Evolution," which does not appear in the subsequent editions of the work. In it he said: " If it be assumed that what we call chemical elements are absolutely simple (which is, however, a hypothesis having no better warrant than the opposite one), then it must be admitted that in respect of the number of kinds of matter contained in it the earth is not more heterogeneous than it was at first—that in this respect it would be as heterogeneous were all its undecomposable parts uniformly mixed, as it is now, when they are arranged and combined in countless different ways. But the increase of heterogeneity with which we have to deal, and of which alone our own senses can take cognisance, is that produced from unity of distribution to variety of distribution. Given an aggregate consisting of several orders of primitive units that were unchangeable, then these units may be so uniformly dispersed among each other that any portion of the mass shall be like any other portion in its sensible properties ; or they may be so segregated, simply and in endless combinations, that the various portions of the mass shall not be like each other in their sensitive properties." (First edition, pp. 335, 336.) We do not mean to dwell on this statement. We quote it merely for its historic interest, and for the proof it gives that Mr. Spencer had once present to his mind the problem of the existence of a homogeneity made up of a number of different kinds of units. Whether he has found it would not work we cannot say ; but we ought to take his final statement as in his view the only adequate one, and to deal with it.

We shall therefore not deal with that discarded

chapter, though the difficulty remains. We shall look at the chemical aspects of the case, and see what a wondrous world chemistry opens to our view—what a rational world of order, adjustments, adaptations it is. " There are different elements," says Faraday, " with the most manifold powers and the most opposite tendencies. Some are so lazy and inert that a superficial observer would take them for nothing in the grand resultant of powers ; and others, on the contrary, possess such violent properties that they seem to threaten the stability of the universe. But on a deeper examination of the rôle which they play, one finds that they agree with one another in a great scheme of harmonic adaptation. The power of no single element could be changed without at once destroying the harmonious balance, and plunging the whole into ruin." (Quoted by Professor Bowne, in *The Philosophy of Herbert Spencer*, pp. 225, 226. Phillips & Hunt : New York.) There are two possible ways of dealing with this scheme of harmonious adaptation. We may accept it as a fact, and deal with it as ultimate ; or we may ask for an explanation of it. In the former event we may proceed to deal with the various elements, seek to ascertain their properties, and their relations to one another and to the whole, and ask no ultimate questions about them. This is precisely what the science of chemistry has done, and is doing. It takes the different elements, and it finds that they resist further decomposition. It enumerates these elements. It has found that the total mass of the substances taking part in any chemical process remains constant, and that the substances consist of very small particles of different kinds, which alter their arrangement and not their nature during any chemical process. It is driven to assume that the atoms of every pure substance are all alike among themselves. If every atom of any given substance is like every other atom, then all the relations of mass in chemical compounds must be regulated by the masses of the several atoms. "All substances consist of discrete particles of finite but very small size—of atoms. Undecomposable substances or elements contain atoms of the same nature, form, mass. If chemical combination takes place between several elements, the atoms of these so arrange themselves that a definite and usually small number of atoms of the combining element form a compound atom which we call a molecule. Every molecule of a definite chemical compound (chemical species) contains the same number of elementary atoms arranged in the same way. If the same elements can unite to form different compounds, the elementary atoms composing the molecules of the latter are either present in different numbers, or, if their number be the same, they are differently arranged." (Ostwald, pp. 7, 8.)

Thus we have to deal not with the permutations and combinations of sixty-seven (the number of elements known at present) different bodies taken in any order, but with something far more wonderful and far more complex. The various elements insist on conditions in choosing partners. With some they refuse to combine at all, and they will never unite with any except on certain terms, and these conditions are fixed and unchangeable.

There is nothing arbitrary either in the elements or in the conditions under which they act. The proportions in which elements unite together are definite and constant, and a given compound always consists of the same elements united in the same proportions. If the elements combine together in several proportions, the several proportions in which the one element unites with the other invariably bear a simple relation to one another. This is the law of combination in multiple proportions. The proportions in which two elements combine with a third also represent the proportion in which, or in some simple multiple of which, they will themselves combine. This is the law of reciprocal proportion.

These three laws, which have been deduced entirely from experimental observations, may be considered as themselves the consequences of the atomic theory. Assume the atomic theory, and these laws can be explained. It is not necessary to discuss the atomic theory here, or even to describe it at any length. The values of the atomic weights are determined only relatively—that is, in reference to the atomic weight of one of the elements assumed as unity. The relative weights of many of the atoms have thus been determined, and the result reveals a scheme of great beauty and simplicity; for it appears that the properties of the elements are periodic functions of their atomic weights. "If all the elements are arranged in the order of their atomic weights in a series, their properties will so vary from member to member that after a definite number of elements have been passed either the first or very similar will recur"

(Ostwald, p. 35). In virtue of this law, and making use of the regularities disclosed by it, Mendelejeff was able to predict the properties of unknown elements from those of their neighbours in the table of atomic weights he had drawn up. " He gave especially a somewhat detailed description of scandium, gallium, germanium, and their components, none of which were known at the time he wrote his memoir ; and to him, as well as to science in general, has been accorded the triumph of seeing these predictions for the most part fulfilled on the subsequent discovery of the elements " (p. 37),—a work to be compared with that of Leverrier and Adams in their discovery of the unknown planet.

As we follow the guidance of the chemists the scheme of harmonic adaptation becomes ever more wonderful ; but we have taken quite enough for the problem now in hand. The harmonious adaptation is there, and every one can see it who chooses to look. If the relation of equality so impressed Clerk Maxwell as to cause him to give utterance to the remark already quoted, what shall we say of the relations now disclosed ? Shall we just accept them as facts, work out their results, and say nothing further about them ? That is one way, and a very useful way it is. It is quite a competent thing for a chemist to do. He may legitimately decline to be troubled with ultimate questions on the plea that he has quite enough to do. It is not a legitimate procedure on the part of the evolutionist, unless he means to give up his task at the outset. Here is the problem set to him. Here are sixty-seven different kinds of bodies, each of which possesses certain properties, each of which is distinct from the rest, and yet related to them in certain definite ways : how are we to account for them ? They are simply given. We cannot make them or unmake. If they were ever other than they now are, that time is long past. They were there when that process of change which men call evolution began, and they are present and operative in every further change : what, then, are we to say about them ? They exist in rational relations, they form combinations which can be thought, and these combinations increase till they form a world. Why should they always unite in definite proportions, and these proportions exist in an intelligible form ? Shall we say they are so, and that we can give no further account of the matter ? That is an intelligible position. The position, however, cannot, we repeat, be taken by any one who professes to give a rational account of the world. If he takes these elements simply as given, then he has failed. If he tries to explain them, then the explanation must be adequate. The persistence of force, the instability of the homogeneous, will not account for the elements in the scheme, or for the scheme itself, as we have already seen. " Abstract notions," said Bishop Butler, " can do nothing "; and the persistence of force is simply an abstract notion that can do nothing till it parts with its abstraction and gets itself translated into the concrete energies of the world as we know it. How did the order, the intelligibility, the rationality of the scheme get into the atoms ? One can understand how the order, the intelligibility, the rationality got into the works on chemistry lying now on the table ;

for the rationality is in Ostwald, in Williamson, in
Armstrong first, and in the books next; but the
order, the rationality, the intelligibility of the atoms
and the system they serve to produce are vastly
greater than those of the systems in the books. Are
we to say that the order of the universe is in no
way related to intelligence? That is a large order.
Is it a great or an unjustifiable assumption to make,
that intelligibility is related to intelligence? We
know that the relation exists in our own case. The
intelligibility of the world is related to the intelligence
which understands it. The intelligibility of a book
has at least two references—one to the author of it,
and another to the reader of it. Shall we say that
the intelligibility of the world has only one reference,
namely, to the reader of it? On what grounds shall
we make the assertion? It can be only on the ground
that we can explain the intelligibility apart from
intelligence.

What has to be accounted for is the unity of all
these chemical elements in one system. As conceived
by science it is a rational system. We shall not
attempt to measure the toil, the perseverance, the
intelligence of the successive generations of chemists
who have slowly built up the magnificent temple
known by the name of chemistry. No one questions
the fact that intelligence has built up science; but
it is to be observed that science has not made the
facts, nor the order, nor the system: it has simply
interpreted what it found. The order, the system,
the rationality are there, in the facts disclosed to
them in the chemical elements and their relations.

They did not make the facts, they found them.   They assumed the rationality of nature, and they found on examination that it was there.   What right had men to assume the rationality of nature?   Why should they have presupposed that the irrational was untrue, that the absurd was impossible? and why should the assumption turn out to be correct?   The only answer is that nature is intelligible, because intelligence was present in it from the beginning.

This form of the argument is of a different kind from the argument from final causes.   Purpose we shall have to look at by-and-by.   But at present we are engaged with efficient causes, with the facts of order, of intelligibility, of interpretability; and one proposition is that order implies intelligence.   So strongly is this felt by many minds at the present hour, that we have any number of hypotheses to account for it.   We have Professor Clifford's hypothesis of mind-stuff: "a moving molecule of inorganic matter possesses a small piece of mind-stuff."   We have the supposition of the cell-soul, of unconscious will, of unconscious intelligence, of the double-faced unity, and of many similar ways of bringing in intelligence as the source of order.   The necessity is felt, and the schemes for bringing in intelligence in some form at some stage are vouched for by the various hypotheses.   The need is sufficiently apparent.   Not to speak, at this stage, of the fact that intelligence has somehow emerged, we content ourselves with the need of accounting for the intelligibility of the chemical system.   To account for its rational order apart from energising reason seems a hopeless task.

We might here avail ourselves of the help of Mr. Spencer did we know how to use it. We might use that part of his philosophy which affirms the existence of a Power, which is manifested in the universe, which he calls " an infinite and eternal Energy from which all things proceed " (*Principles of Sociology*, p. 843). He tells us also " that the Power manifested throughout the universe distinguished as material is the same power which in ourselves wells up under the form of consciousness " (p. 839). We also believe in that Power. But that Power appears in Mr. Spencer's system on very rare occasions. The actual changes in the universe, which he calls by the name of evolution, are in the hands of deputies. The formula of evolution reveals as much. " Evolution is an integration of matter and concomitant dissipation of motion, during which the matter passes from an indefinite, incoherent homogeneity to a definite, coherent heterogeneity ; and during which the retained motion undergoes a parallel transformation " (*First Principles*, p. 396). It may be that matter and motion are themselves only symbolic, as Mr. Spencer says they are. But the fact remains that they are the only symbols through which the unknowable Power is permitted by Mr. Spencer to act. All the process of evolution is worked out by Mr. Spencer on these terms and by these symbols. It is limited by them, and can use no other. Thus we can get no help from Mr. Spencer for the solution of our limited problem. Granted that the unknowable Power is the source of that complex order which we find in the chemical system, yet that does not carry us far; for we have no explanation of that integration of matter which we have observed in the chemical elements. They do not belong to the present constitution of things. Nor have we any explanation of the fact that these elements exist in relations which can be thought. We get Power from Mr. Spencer, but we get it simply as unknowable, and that is a form, or want of form, which we cannot use. If, however, Mr. Spencer postulates a Power behind the process of evolution, if he can affirm the existence of an infinite and eternal Energy from which all things proceed, there is no reason why we should not follow so good an example. We also have a right to assume a Power behind or within the chemical elements, which will help us to account for the orderly and complex relations in which they exist. We already are acquainted with a power of that kind. We know intelligence as the source of order; we are acquainted with the way in which a principle of intelligence may be impressed on a number of efficient causes, and may cause them to exist as an intelligible system. At present we are not discussing the seat of the intelligence impressed on a material system. The intelligence may be within the system, or it may be without the system; it may be immanent or transcendent; the discussion is quite irrelevant to the main question, which is intelligence as the source of order. We have a *vera causa* adequate to the production of the result, and the alternative seems to lie between this explanation and no explanation.

But, then, the system of chemistry does manifest

intelligence. In this fact lies our advantage, and we
mean to make full use of it, and to press it home.
We have adjustments, adaptations, relations, which
reveal themselves to the person who attends to them,
and these are not merely mechanical. The argument
becomes more stringent and more incisive as we pass
beyond the merely chemical world into the wider
world which it subserves. The more complex the
arrangements become, the greater does the demand
for intelligence become. One step beyond the atoms,
and we come to the phenomena presented by water.
It is but a step, and yet what a step ! Oxygen and
hydrogen are the constituent elements of water.
They combine in certain proportions, which are in-
variable. The molecule of water is relatively stable,
and its two elements can be separated only when
work is done on them. Yet this material of water
evolved at one step has many of the most wonderful
properties—properties which fit it to play a great
part in the economy of the universe. Take its point
of maximum density, and observe how it is related
to the part which it plays in the world. From that
point 4° C. it expands when heated, and expands also
when cooled. It takes more heat to warm it than
any other body, and can therefore give more heat out
when it cools. Archdeacon Wilson asks what would
an architect give for a heating apparatus which would
convey heat from one part of the world to another,
and itself remain cool. Yet he says aqueous vapour
is doing it every day of our lives. But all these
things flow from the properties of water ! That is
exactly what we are saying. These properties are

given, with all their results, and they are in relation to the material universe in which they are. They, however, raise the question of how they became what they are. The properties of oxygen and hydrogen are unlike the properties of water. They have separately properties which it has not, and it has properties which they have not. We get no explanation out of the physical powers by which water had its origin. Even when we have traced its meaning, we are still at a loss for the explanation. Is it not evident that here again we must have recourse to intelligence as the source of order?

As we follow our teachers in science from one science to another, and watch the revelation of order more and more involved and intricate, yet all, in the end, embraced in the unity of one system, we are lost in admiration and in awe. The rationality of the system becomes the more apparent as we advance. The world is a rational world, and we see no reason on that account to deny rationality to the Power from which all things proceed. If we grant intelligence to that power, then evolution becomes luminous; refuse to grant it, and we must simply regard the order as an ultimate fact, and say no more about it.

But it may be said that here we are postulating a cause less complex than the effect, and are, in short, acting on the Spencerian maxim that the cause is always less complex than the effect. It is not so, for intelligence is in itself not simple, but complex; and besides, the objection does not apply to intelligence, because of the very nature and work of it. It is the very nature of intelligence to bring many unrelated elements into a synthetic unity. Even our own intelligence brings all the objects of its experience into the unity of one space and one time. Intelligence can bring many elements into the unity of one system. If intelligence of the limited order we know in ourselves can impress itself on a number of unrelated things, and make them exist in the unity of one system, what may not an infinite intelligence be able to accomplish !

CHAPTER IV

THE STRIFE AGAINST PURPOSE

Is the issue raised by evolution new or old?—Scope of evolution—Is evolution self-explanatory?—Fiske on teleology, against and for: order and purpose—Efficient and final causes—Caprice—Spinoza on final causes—Mathematics—Purposiveness—The same facts and laws appear from the point of view of cause and of purpose—Chance or purpose.

WE are to devote this chapter to the inquiry whether the issue raised by evolution is one which is new, or is the issue one which has been tried over and over again during the history of human thought? We admit at once that the theory of evolution has cast new light on the universe, and has made the problem at once more complex and more simple. We have to reckon with evolution in every department. Du Prel says : " In the progress of modern science no principle has proved so fruitful as that of evolution. All branches compete with one another in its use, and have brought about by its aid the most gratifying results. Geology interprets the significance of superimposed, hardened strata of the earth's crust in the sense of a history of the earth's development; biology, in union with the study of fossils, arranges the living and petrified specimens of plants and animals in their order, and constructs a history of the evolution of organic life; philology prepares a genealogical tree of languages, and finds in it signs which throw light on prehistoric times and reveal facts forgotten for thousands of years; anthropology discovers in the form and expression of human beings rudimentary signs that point to a theory of development from lower forms; and finally history reveals the evolution of civilisation in far-distant historic times; and in all these branches it becomes apparent that we only then understand phenomena when we have comprehended their becoming." (Quoted from *A Review of Evolutional Ethics*, by Charles Williams, pp. 274, 275.) The description is not exaggerated. All workers in science now simply assume evolution, on the hypothesis of evolution they proceed, by the questions it raises research and investigation are directed, and by the light of it every fresh discovery is read. Thus by the method it prescribes, by the questions it asks, and by the results it has won, evolution holds the field.

While we clearly admit all this, we have still something to say. There is still the question to be asked, What is implied in evolution? Is it a self-explanatory process? Is it a process which can dispense with a marshalling and directing agency? Is it a system or a method which can get on without the guidance of intelligence, or proceed without the assumption of purpose? We may take the statement of the issue from Mr. Fiske : " From the dawn of philosophic discussion, Pagan and Christian, Trinitarian and Deist have appealed to the harmony pervading nature as the surest foundation of their faith in an intelligent and beneficent Ruler of the universe. We meet with the argument in the familiar writings of Xenophon and Cicero, and it is forcibly and eloquently maintained by Voltaire as well as by Paley, by Agassiz as well as by the authors of the *Bridge-water Treatises*. One and all they challenge us to explain, on any other hypothesis than that of creative design, these manifold harmonies, these exquisite adaptations of means to ends, whereof the world is admitted to be full, and which are especially conspicuous among the phenomena of life. Until the establishment of the doctrine of evolution, the glove thus thrown, age after age, into the arena of philosophic controversy, was never triumphantly taken up. It was Mr. Darwin who first, by his discovery of natural selection, supplied the champions of science with the resistless weapon by which to vanquish, in this their chief stronghold, the champions of theology." (*Cosmic Philosophy*, vol. ii., pp. 396, 397.) Mr. Fiske was enthusiastic and very confident when he wrote those words. About twenty years ago some men were enthusiastic about evolution. They felt they had found the key to make every mystery plain, to solve every problem, and they spent a good deal of time in proving how triumphant they were. Some people also were in a panic. They felt as if the old, old controversy had come to an end, that they were left to a universe in which there was no shaping intelligence, no directing agency, nothing akin to themselves in the vast spaces of the universe. By-and-by calmer counsels prevailed. Enthusiasms wore out, and panic died away. As they became better acquainted with the claim and scope of evolution, they came to see that matters were very much as of old. Professor Huxley came to see and to say that theology had not received its death-blow, and Mr. Fiske lived to write as follows : " The teleological instinct in man cannot be suppressed or ignored. The human soul shrinks from the thought that it is without kith or kin in all this wide universe. Our reason demands that there shall be a reasonableness in the constitution of things. This demand is a fact in our psychical nature as positive and as irrepressible as our acceptance of geometrical axioms and our rejection of whatever controverts such axioms. No ingenuity of argument can bring us to believe that the infinite Sustainer of the universe will put us to permanent intellectual confusion. There is in every earnest thinker a craving after a final cause ; and this craving can no more be extinguished than our belief in objective reality. Nothing can persuade us that the universe is a farrago of nonsense. Our belief in what we call the evidence of our senses is less strong than our faith in the orderly sequence of events : there is a meaning which our minds could fathom were they only vast enough." (*The Idea of God*, pp. 137, 138.)

It is curious to look back for twenty years, and to read the literature of that time over again. The tone of triumph is as marked on the one side as the note of depression and of pain is on the other. To-day, except in some quarters, the triumph and the panic have both subsided, as it has done in former instances of the same kind. We may note the same kind of elation and depression following on every great discovery in science. And it seemed to be founded on the notion that wherever the presence of law was discovered there was also proved the absence of God. Strange to say, the discovery of gravitation was held to be a disproof of the existence of God. Physicists said it, and theologians feared it. In connection with physics, in connection with the advance of chemistry, with geology, and with the advance of almost every science, there has been a period of elation and of depression. So with evolution, which, if true, is the largest advance yet made by the mind of man, and consequently enthusiasm rose to a great height, and depression fell correspondingly low.

The issue raised is really the old issue between the atomists of Greece and those who postulated mind as a true cause. It is the issue between Lucretius on the one hand, and, say, Cicero on the other. It is raised also in its most classical form by Spinoza ; and it could not but be raised wherever order, regularity have been discovered. The difference to-day is that the issue is raised with more knowledge on either side. On the one hand, science has a wider knowledge of law, a more accurate understanding of physical causation, a more rigid adherence to the persuasion that there is nothing in the universe which is not under law, and law and order have a wider meaning. But, on the other hand, theology has come to understand better what it means by God. It has been able to separate from the idea of God everything like caprice, arbitrariness, whimsicality. From its idea of God it has banished those elements of uncertainty which drove Lucretius to distraction and tortured the higher mind of Greece. Both sides have come to see that law, order, regularity are indispensable ; and the question has come to be, What is implied in the thought of an orderly universe, moving under law ? Can order explain itself ? Can a system of efficient causes account for itself ?

It surely ought not to be difficult to come to an understanding. Theologians can surely say with Tyndall that theology as well as " science demands the radical extirpation of caprice, and the absolute reliance upon law in nature." Theology surely has no interest in the maintenance of caprice. She is conscious that her position is misrepresented by Leon Dumont, if he means to say that her view is that which he denounces. " If the existence of a superior intelligence can be demonstrated by physical proofs, it is not by the spectacle of order and regularity, but merely by abnormal and contradictory facts, in a word, by miracle." Another says : " The scientific sense of the term law is utterly opposed to that of will. Will in the only intelligible sense of which we have any knowledge, namely, human will, is vengeful, arbitrary, variable, capricious." Theologians have an interest in making our scientific men know that by will they do not mean caprice, that by purpose they do not mean arbitrariness. The will they postulate as the ultimate source of things is a will which is the cause of order and law in the universe, a will which is steadfast and unchangeable, conscious of itself and its purpose, foreseeing the end, and taking means to bring it about. When we speak of purpose, we do not mean intermeddling with things for the sake of caprice. When we speak of purpose in the universe, we just imply that the universe has a meaning, that the system of efficient causes is in the grasp of a final cause.

The controversy which we have with such men as Mr. Spencer, Mr. Fiske in his cosmic philosophy, is merely that they have an inadequate notion of causation, that they attribute to the effect more than there is in the cause. They shut us out from any consideration of purpose, and compel us to try to deduce all things from the system of efficient causes, even when these are plainly inadequate for the purpose. Why should we be compelled to try to understand the universe by a process which shuts out more than one half of the best elements of our thinking? We know no reason save the dread which the scientific man has of caprice. But we have seen that caprice can have no place in an infinite, eternal, and unchangeable Mind, who knows itself and its purpose. Why should we be forced to say where we see a system of causes working out an intelligible end that this end was neither foreseen nor intended? But perhaps we ought to look at the classical exposition of the subject.

In the first book of the Ethics, Spinoza develops the thesis that all things are predetermined by God, not through His free will or absolute fiat, but from the very nature of God as infinite power. Having determined that all possible things are real, and all real things are necessary, in the appendix he makes a strenuous attack on the teleological exposition of the

world : that God directs all things to a definite goal.
"For it is said that God made all things for man, and
man that he might worship Him." He sets himself
first to show how this view obtains general credence,
and, second, he points out its falsity. Men are
conscious of their desires and volitions, and unconscious of the causes which disposed them to wish and
desire. Men do all things for an end, and therefore
they only look for a knowledge of the final causes of
events; and when these are learned they are content,
as having no cause for further doubt. " Further, as
they find in themselves and outside themselves many
means which assist them not a little in their search
for what is useful—for instance, eyes for seeing, teeth
for chewing, herbs and animals for yielding food, the
sun for giving light, the sea for breeding fish, etc.—
they come to look on the whole of nature as a means
for obtaining such conveniences. Now, as they are
aware that they found such conveniences and did not
make them, they think they have cause for believing
that some other being has made them for their use.
As they look upon things as means, they cannot believe
them to be self-created; and judging from the means
they are accustomed to prepare for themselves, they
are bound to believe in some ruler of the universe
endowed with human freedom, who has arranged and
adapted them for human use." (Elwes' translation,
vol. ii., p. 76.) Spinoza thinks that nature has no
particular goal in view, and that final causes are
human figments. There is another standard of verity,
and that is the standard set up by mathematics,
which considers solely the essence and properties of

figures without regard to their final causes. When the notion of final cause is dismissed, along with it go all those conceptions which presuppose the idea of purpose, such as goodness, badness, order, confusion, warmth, cold, beauty, and deformity. These are rooted in the fortuitous interests and the varying tastes of the individual, and are mere abstract notions framed for the explanation of the nature of things.

These are some of the maxims by which Spinoza sought to destroy the idea of purpose. Not since Lucretius had such an assault been made on teleology. The influence of Spinoza's assault can be traced, and it has been operative from his day to ours. At the same time, it may be questioned whether Spinoza has put the case fairly, or rightly set forth the distinction between mathematical and other knowledge. He admits that men " come to look on the whole of nature as a means for obtaining such conveniences," and men "found these conveniences and did not make them"; in other words, there was some objective justification for their taking that view. At present we are not concerned with the adequacy of Spinoza's representation of the teleological judgment. It is true that he has misrepresented it ; but, even on his own showing, there is a correspondence between the nature of the world and man's way of looking at the world teleologically. This is implied in the statement, "they found these conveniences and did not make them "; in other words, this way of looking at things is related to reality.

His statement applies with much more force to mathematics. At first we do not know whether our

mathematical judgments have any relation to a real
world. They may be figments of the imagination;
for in all geometrical figures I actually make a bounding of space by a rule of my own, and I do not know
that anything real corresponds to that bounding. I
assume that space may be bounded; but whether it
really can be thus bounded I do not know until I
ascertain. I imagine a point to move at the same
distance from a fixed point, and I call the boundary
thus traced out a circle. From it I can deduce any
number of propositions. It enables me to say that
the line joining the vertices of all triangles, having
the same base and the same vertical angle, is a
circle. We can deal with conic sections in the same
way. At first men could not say of what use such
studies might be. The old geometers proceeded with
such investigations, and never asked of what use their
propositions and deductions might be. They worked
out the properties of the parabola, the ellipse, and the
hyperbola, and they never asked where there were
any bodies in nature whose movements corresponded
to the curves whose properties they investigated.
They did not think that real bodies in space might
move in ellipses, nor that a central force varied
according to the inverse square of the distance. For
all they knew these curves might or might not have
a reference to reality. It was a science of imagination,
based on the intuition of space and time, and on the
laws of deductive logic. And mathematics has
not furnished the standard of verity which Spinoza
demanded. For in the first instance mathematics
reveals only the nature of the human mind with its

intuitions, its power of reasoning, and its conformity to the laws of logic. Mathematics shows how the human mind works when under few and simple conditions. It is a witness to the power and the rationality of the human mind, and that is all that can be said about it.

"It is quite different if I meet with order and regularity in complexes of *things* external to myself, enclosed within real boundaries, as, *e.g.*, in a garden the order and regularity of the trees, flower-beds, and walks. These I cannot expect to derive *a priori* from my bounding of space made after a rule of my own; for this order and regularity are existing things which must be given empirically in order to be known, and not a mere representation of myself determined *a priori* according to a principle." (Kant, *Kritik of Judgment*, Bernard's translation, p. 205.) Thus the question is, How are we related to reality? Mathematics regards only what is possible; and after we have elaborated it, the further question arises, How far does reality conform to mathematics? We have still to ask, How far do things empirically given conform to our way of looking at them? If concrete things, real things in a real world, behave as our ideal points behave when they describe the triangles, circles, conic sections of our mathematics, then may we not say that an intelligence is at work in the world akin to the intelligence which was at work in the construction of our mathematics? If our intuition and our logic are realised in nature, and if nature works out our mathematics in a grander, more thorough way than we can, then surely the inference is quite plain.

Nature is the work of an intelligence that knows mathematics.

Is teleology, then, hostile to science? Let us see what the scientific interest is. The scientific interest is in any given subject to find out not only what it is, but why it is so and so. This interest is satisfied when we can point out the causes through which it has become. Science does not inquire into the origin of causes, nor into the ground of their universal worth : it is satisfied when the applicability of the given causes to produce this particular result is shown. What science presupposes is a given manifoldness of things, substances, atoms, forces, etc., which have definite and defined qualities, and these so related to one another as to make the result necessary. When two masses in space are at a particular distance from one another, their movements necessarily follow from their mass and their distance. When two bodies strike against one another, the resulting movement is determined by their weight, their velocity, their elasticity. Causes therefore, according to science, are things with their properties and forces, and these are given. When these are given, results necessarily follow ; and necessity in nature corresponds to that inner necessity with which we are acquainted, the necessity by which a conclusion follows from given premises. The necessity of nature is also an intellectual necessity.

It is to be observed also that the point of departure in science is always a defined group of things which work and are worked on. Out of a thing considered in itself no change can come; forces are the expression of the changes of related substances; all causes for science are external causes. Work done presupposes a manifoldness of things in defined relations. From the given condition at this moment we work back to its condition some time before, and then comes a point at which we must stop. Science has found its limit. Our intuitions, our logical necessities have their counterpart in nature. May not our way of looking at things as means and ends have its counterpart in nature just as our way of looking at things as cause and consequence has? May not purpose also be a finer and more unique kind of necessity?

The idea of purpose no doubt arises out of our voluntary and practical activity. Our conscious activity is determined by the thought of the future. This thought influences our will, our will determines our activity, which is directed towards the realisation of our thought, and a course of conduct arises. This relation to a future event to be realised in conduct is the distinctive characteristic of purpose. Purpose is, however, not merely subjective; it is not a mere wish which does not issue in action : it sets itself to find means to realise itself; it quickens the intelligence, and sets itself to make use of real, efficient causes, and so arrange them as to bring about the foreseen result. Purpose remains mere wish until it can link itself to the real working causes of the world, and make use of or make a mechanism to give it effect. Purpose, first a thought in the mind, becomes active, and sets the mind and will to work; it sets the mechanism of the body to work, and so finally the mechanism of the mind is controlled, and made to act in order to bring about a result which mechanism could never of itself have produced. Purpose, then, has a real place as far at least as human action is regarded. Everywhere we see a purpose impressed on systems of efficient causes. We see machines, ships, steam engines, telephones, telegraphs, everywhere at work, and they are possible because systems of efficient causes are receptive of purpose. There are two ways of considering a steam engine. We may look at it as a system of efficient causes, and investigate the properties and relations of the various elements contained in it, and try to understand the mechanical theory of the steam engine. We work synthetically from the causes to the result. But we may legitimately work from another point of view, and take the result as our point of departure. We may ask through which combination of causes was this result produced ; and from this point of view the result appears as purpose, and the working causes appear as means by which the purpose was realised. We may look at the solar system, and regard the stability of the system as the result of the movements of the planets in the same direction, and so on ; but it is also a legitimate way to look at the stability of the system first, and at all the co-ordinated movements as means which serve to realise that end. Are we told that the postulating of such a purpose is hypothetical ? But we cannot get rid of the hypothetical element. One course of procedure says, if such and such causes are given, then the result must be so and so ; and the other course says, if this result has come, then the causes must be so and so. The same laws and causes come into observation from both points of view. If we look at an event as a realised purpose, we bring also into view the system of causes which was used to realise the end, and the system of causes is the same as that which brings about the event considered merely as an event apart from purpose. Were our knowledge more thorough, were it only complete, we might read the order of the universe backwards and forwards— backwards to a system of efficient causes, and forwards to a defined and predetermined end. But our knowledge is far from complete, and therefore we object to an arbitrary decision on the part of many, a decision which shuts us out from a fruitful way of looking at the universe, merely because we do not know enough to carry out that view in its application to all the details of the universe.

We may not be able to say what is the purpose of an eclipse; we may rest content with the knowledge that in certain relations of the movements of the earth, the moon, and the sun, eclipses of the moon or the sun will happen periodically. That is merely to say that our knowledge is not great enough for us to set all the events of the universe in the light of purpose. It might be possible for us to deny efficient causation on the same ground, because there are many spheres in which we have not yet been able to say what the causation really is. But the denial of purpose in nature is simply an appeal to ignorance; or if our adversaries wish to be scornful, they call it anthropomorphism. And they ask us, Are we to conceive the power which rules the universe working after the fashion of a man? We have dealt with anthropomorphism elsewhere (*Is God Knowable?* chap. iii.), and we shall not repeat here what we have formerly written. Is not the mathematical thinking of the universe done after the fashion of a man? Are not the ellipses, the parabolas of the Greek geometers patterns according to which the planets move? Is not the necessity of nature paralleled by the necessity of logic? Both in nature and in logic what is absurd is impossible. The system of efficient causes which we find at work in the world is just as anthropomorphic as the system of final causes is. The spectacle of a human intelligence working for a foreseen end, finding out what causes can be disposed and in what way for the accomplishment of that end, is as real, as grand, as much related to nature and reality as is the same intelligence working out its geometry, its algebra, its calculus by the laws of logic, deducing its great propositions from a few elementary axioms. If we accept the logical necessity of the universe, even though it be anthropomorphic, why on that ground deny its purposiveness?

Given a certain state of matters, how may we explain it? Given a human work, be it a machine, a song, a book, a theory of gravitation or of evolution, and we can explain it by a reference to the author, his intelligence, and his purpose. We may take into account the material of which the machine is composed, as we take into account the paper, type, ink, etc., of which the book is composed ; we may inquire into the qualities and laws of the given material ; but in the end we say the explanation of the product is

5

the author. In evolution the matter to be explained is the universe. Is it best explained by purpose or by mechanism? As we have seen, mechanism cannot explain it. Most certainly the primitive nebulosity cannot explain it; for the nebulists are confronted with the following dilemma: either the nebula was originally more than a nebula, or it has been added to, in the course of its development, from a source beyond itself. The effect cannot be greater than the cause. If the primitive nebulosity has become the ordered cosmos with all its inhabitants, art, science, philosophy, morality, religions must all have been either in the nebula at first, or added to it from without by a power adequate to the result. Power, either within the nebula or from without, there must have been, and power of a kind fitted to bring about the end. Let it be observed that the chain of ordered causes and results is the same, whether we contemplate it from the point of view of physical causation or from the point of view of purpose. In the one case we contemplate it as bare result, in the other case we look at it as intended, and the ordered causes are grouped together with a view to accomplish the end. In the last event we have a cause sufficient to bring about the result; in the former case we have no account whatever of the order, adaptation, and method of the universe. We must go back to the fortuitous concourse of atoms, and trust to chance— to chance, now, be it remembered, not as a name for a cause the operation and nature of which we do not know now, but may hope to know by-and-by, but to chance looked at as a real cause. It may be allowed to speak of chance as an element in a calculation of probabilities simply to express ignorance ; but it is not allowable to speak of chance as a substitute for causation, and to this we are brought if we deny purpose in the universe.

But we give the universe over to confusion when we deny purpose. " You would not see evidence of purpose, we are told, much less of higher wisdom or transcendent cleverness, in the conduct of a man who, to kill a hare, fired a million pistols in all directions over a vast meadow ; or who, to enter a locked room, brought ten thousand random keys, and made trial of them all; or who, to have a house, built a city, and turned the superfluous houses over to the mercy of wind and weather." And to this we are brought by our antagonism to what Mr. Spencer calls the Carpenter theory. Notwithstanding the description of Lange just given, Mr. Spencer writes : " There is an antagonistic hypothesis which does not propose to honour the unknown Power manifested in the universe by such titles as ' the Master Builder,' or ' the great Artificer '; but which regards this un-known Power as probably working after a method quite different from that of human mechanics. And the genealogy of this hypothesis is as high as that of the other is low. It is begotten by that ever-enlarging and ever-strengthening belief in the presence of law which accumulated experiences have gradually produced in the human mind. From generation to generation science has been proving uniformities of relation among phenomena which were before thought either fortuitous or supernatural in their origin—has been showing an established order and a constant causation where ignorance had assumed irregularity and arbitrariness.   Each further discovery of law has increased the presumption that law is everywhere conformed to." (*Essays*, vol. i., p. 240.)   Lange and Professor Huxley would overthrow design by likening the survival of the fittest to the chance shot which out of a million happened to kill the hare.   Mr. Spencer would overthrow it by showing that law everywhere prevails.   But the idea of law and uniformity is also quite consistent with the idea of purpose.   In fact, purpose excludes arbitrariness and irregularity, and any assertion to the contrary is simply itself capricious.

CHAPTER V

EVOLUTION AND CREATION

History of the earth—Evolution as seen in geologic eras—
Continuity of the process—Succession—Advance and
preparation for advance—Physics and geology—Some
unsettled questions—Professor Caird on evolution from
two points of view—At the beginning or at the end,
which?—Is the issue arbitrary arrangement *versus* evolution?—No : creation by slow process is creation—Illustrations—Mechanics and purpose once more.

THAT teleology is not hostile to efficient causes
we have already seen reason to believe. Still
less does it conflict with efficient causes combined in a
system. In fact, as we advance along the line of march
which science has taken, the idea of teleology becomes
more and more luminous, until in ethics and theology
it becomes indispensable. We quite admit that the
idea is anthropomorphic, that it does not quite enable
us to view all things *sub specie eternitatis*. We admit
that we are unable to rise to the great height of one
who is present at all the operations of the world, for
whom beginning and end are not, to whom all time
is a *nunc stans*. But, then, that objection applies to
every one who is compelled to think under the conditions of space and time, and applies equally to those
who affirm causation of any kind. Efficient causes

also come under the condition of before and after; and if to think of efficient causation is valid and legitimate, final causation is also valid and legitimate.

We might therefore start with the state of the earth as it now is, and might ask what are the conditions under which rational life can exist at the present time. We might analyse these conditions, and the analysis would give us at least the various sciences in the order in which they now exist. The present condition would give us the previous conditions, biological, geological, chemical, physical, ranged in order and complexity, as each was analysed into simpler and simpler elements, and not one of the laws of nature would need to be altered in order to make the arrangement. Nothing is changed save the point of view. The difference is that we do not start with the nebula, and endeavour, by successive differentiations and integrations, to get out of it more than is in it. We start with the present state of the world as an intended result, and look on all the successive stages of the life-history of the earth as means for the accomplishment of the end.

True, we are at a disadvantage here; for the world is not finally made yet. It is only making, and we can only dimly guess at the final outcome. But, then, all schemes of thought are open to the same objection. Evolution itself, in the hands of Mr. Spencer, can only faintly guess at the final end for which evolution works. And Hegel's theory of evolution seemed to regard the Prussian of the nineteenth century as the final outcome of the toil of the Idea. We may hold, therefore, although we do not know the final outcome of things, that the power which has brought the nebula to the stage where life with its thought, its morality, and religion exists in the earth, will continue to work in such a way as to bring it to further issues yet, and to an end worth all the cost.

Apart from the thought of an end, we really get no sufficient account of the various stages of the life-history of the earth. The path which the course of things has taken seems really indeterminate. It does not seem natural to say that it must have taken the course it did, otherwise force would not have persisted. The persistence of force does not explain the direction in which it persisted. Force persists quite as much in the moon as on the earth, as much in the Sahara as in the city of London, as much in the sand on the sea-shore as in Westminster Abbey. At every point of transition the difficulty arises, Why should the force take this particular path? and apart from intelligent direction and selection we get no answer.

If the nebula theory as a whole finds it difficult to pass from the indeterminate to the determinate, that part of it which applies to our own planet has experienced equal perplexity. We have no agreement among scientists about the time when the earth broke off from the central mass, nor when the earth began to cool, nor when life became possible on its surface. The question is of importance for evolution; for evolution needs time, and a good deal of it. Apart, however, from these difficulties, which we may look at again, we may say geology makes out a magnificent case for evolution. Starting from the earth as a molten mass with a certain motion in its orbit and a certain rotation around its axis, we look at it as cooling according to the rules under which bodies still lose their heat. It is subject to the usual stresses which take place in a body which grows solid as it cools. A crust is formed, and an atmosphere surrounds it, and the older rocks are made. " We can imagine a scum or crust forming at the surface ; and from what we know of the earth's interior, nothing is more likely to have constituted that slaggy crust than the material of our old gneisses. As to its bedded character, this may have arisen in part from the addition of cooler layers below, in part from the action of heated water above, and in part from pressure or tension ; while wherever it cracked or became broken its interstices would be injected with molten matter from beneath. All this may be conjectured, but it is based on known facts, and it is the only probable conjecture. If correct, it would account for the fact that the gneissic rocks are the lowest and oldest that we reach in any part of the earth." (*Salient Points in the Science of the Earth*, pp. 17, 18, by Sir J. William Dawson.)

Geology takes up the study of the earth, and traces for us its evolution. It reveals to us a period of its history when there was no life on its surface ; it shows the earth gradually cooling down, becoming more and more differentiated and integrated under physical laws the working of which is known ; it traces the formation of rocks, the separation of land and water, the formation of an atmosphere, and the gradual formation of these conditions which make life possible. It reveals to us how complex are these conditions, how exquisite are the correlations, how manifold the relations which were needed that this end might be accomplished. The slightest difference in these correlations would make life for ever impossible. Then it shows us the beginnings of life. Life begins in the simplest possible form. It goes on from more to more. Some forms, indeed, remain unchanged almost from the beginning until now. We have still with us the algæ, the mosses, crustaceans, molluscs, and corals of the palæozoic period ; and types which correspond to those forms of life which characterise the mesozoic and the tertiary periods. Under the guidance of science we see life pressing out in all directions, forming new combinations, new types, until the possibility of organic modifications seems exhausted, and a form of being appears who develops a new power of adaptation and does not need to modify himself organically in order to adapt himself to the changing environment. Were we present at all the stages of the process, we should surely see that all the changes were gradual, that the process was slow and continuous. Very likely there was nothing abrupt, nothing catastrophic; everything was prepared for, and every change introduced without violence.

We take the story of geology from our scientific masters, and accept it as they give it. We follow them with no misgiving as they unfold for us the magnificent evolution of the earth's progress throughout geologic time. We know of the difficulties and disagreements between the physicists and the geologists. We know that the uniformitarian in geology demands that the forces acting on the surface of the globe have been in all times the same, both in kind and degree, with those now in operation; and we know that if this is so, a larger amount of time is needed than the physicist can grant. Geologists, however, while agreed as to the kind of forces in operation, are not all uniformitarian with regard to the amount and rate of work which these forces exerted in former times; for if the theory of tidal evolution be true, then the tides once exerted a force on the earth which was immeasurably greater than they exert now. If the earth was ever a molten mass, then the process of cooling, with all the consequent stresses and strains, must have caused effects greater by far than have been experienced since man was upon the earth.

The assumption, then, that the forces operative now were operative throughout all time in the same degree must be departed from, and with it also will go the vast periods of time which Lyall and Darwin demanded as the primary condition of their theory. We are not careful, however, to insist on these difficulties. We leave the differences between physicist and geologist to be settled between them and by them. We refer to them here for the sake of uttering a caveat against the dogmatism of science. The uniformitarian dogma in geology and the partial theories of physicists have been used, not by the masters themselves, but by some others, for the purpose of making attacks on theology and ethics, and it is therefore well to point out that these attacks are premature. There are unsettled questions about the rigidity of the earth, the rate of geologic change, and the date of the introduction of man on the earth; and we are often brought face to face with apparently irreconcilable opinions, held dogmatically by physicists on the one hand and by geologists on the other, and yet the controversial tyro uses these irreconcilable views as if they were in agreement with each other, and thinks he has shown that theology is absurd and religion irrational. On the contrary, we say that theology is prepared to receive whatever science has been able to prove; and if evolution is the law of life, theology will accept evolution as it has accepted gravitation. We accept the fact that physical laws are permanent, but we ask our scientific masters to show us what were the conditions under which the laws were exhibited; and if the conditions change, then the effects will also change.

For the purposes of my argument it is not necessary, however, to make much of these irreconcilable views. Let us accept the general course of the evolution of the earth's history as known. Let us assume that the order was, as is outlined to us by physics and geology so far as they are agreed, first a world without life, next a world with life, then life more and more developed, until we come to the complex life of the present hour; then the question arises,—the only question that has really any significance in the present argument,—How are we to interpret this order? Are we to take our point of view from the beginning or from the end? Are we to say with Professor Caird?— "A principle of development necessarily manifests itself most clearly in the most mature form of that which develops; as we take our definition of man.

not from the embryo or the infant, but from the grown man, who first shows what was hidden in both. . . . When, indeed, we turn back from the developed organism to the embryo, from the man to the child, we find that a study of the process of genesis casts no little light upon the nature of the being which is its result. The man becomes in a higher sense intelligible when we trace him back to the child. But primarily, and in the first instance, it is the developed organism that explains the germ from which it grew; and without having seen the former, we could have made nothing of the latter. No examination of the child could enable us to prophesy the man, if we had not previously had some experience of mature manhood; still less would an examination of the seed in the embryo reveal to us the distinct lineaments of the developed plant, or animal, or man. Nor would our insight be greatly helped by a knowledge of the environment in which the process of development was to take place. . . . Development is not simply the recurrence of the same effects in similar circumstances, not simply the maintenance of an identity under a variation determined by external conditions. Hence it is impossible, from the phenomena of one stage of a developing being, to derive laws which will adequately explain the whole course of its existence. The secret of the peculiar nature of such a being lies just in the way of regular transition in which, by constant interaction with external influences, it widens the compass of its life, unfolding continually new powers and capacities— powers and capacities latent in it from the first, but not capable of being foreseen by one who had seen only the beginning. It follows that, in the first instance at least, we must read development *backward* and not *forward*, we must find the key to the meaning of the first stage in the last; though it is quite true that, afterwards, we are enabled to throw new light upon the nature of the last, to analyse and appreciate it in a new way, by carrying it back to the first." (*Evolution of Religion*, vol. i., pp. 43-5.)

Thus we see there are two ways of interpreting evolution. Limiting our view at present to the globe on which we live, and looking at the history of the earth as now read by science, are we to take our stand at the present time, or are we to go back to the primeval molten globe? Taking our stand at the beginning, we shall be under the necessity of bringing out of the globe all that has since evolved. We shall need an explanation of the tendency and direction which its history really took. It will not suffice to show that such and such events have happened. We have taken on ourselves the burden of showing from the nature of the globe that they could not have happened otherwise. We must be prepared to show that every stage of the process from the beginning until now admits of no alternative. That, however, is a burden too heavy for science to bear. The general laws of matter will never account for particular effects; and the particular arrangements are just the things which need to be explained. Causes and consequences have to be translated into a system of means and ends, if we are to have any intelligible understanding of the process.

The issue is often put thus : Arbitrary arrangement

versus evolution.   But we do not accept the issue in
these terms, for there is no connection between arbitrariness and design.   Speaking of the solar system,
Mr. Spencer says: " When gravitation came to dispense
with these celestial steersmen, there was begotten a
belief, less gross than its parent, but partaking of the
same essential nature, that the planets were launched
in their orbits from the Creator's hand " (*Essays*, i.,
p. 240).   Dr. Romanes puts the issue thus: " Now it
would be proof positive of intelligent design if it could
be shown that all species of planets and animals were
created—that is, *suddenly* introduced into the complex
conditions of their life ; for it is quite inconceivable
that any cause other than intelligence could be
competent to adapt an organism to its environment
suddenly.   On the other hand, it would be proof
presumptive of natural selection if it could be
shown that one species became slowly transmuted
into another—*i.e.*, that one set of adaptations may be
gradually transformed into another set of adaptations according as changing circumstances require.
This would be proof presumptive of natural selection,
because it would then become amply probable that
natural selection might have brought about many,
or most, of the cases of adaptations which we see ;
and if so, the law of parsimony excludes the rival
hypothesis of intelligent design.   Thus the whole
question as between natural selection and supernatural
design resolves itself into this : Were all the species of
plants and animals separately created, or were they
slowly evolved ?   For if they were specially created, the
evidence of supernatural design remains irrefuted and

irrefutable ; whereas, if they were slowly evolved, that evidence has been utterly and for ever destroyed." (*The Scientific Evidences of Organic Evolution*, pp. 12, 13.)

Reserving at present the question of the adequacy of natural selection, we ask, Is the issue fairly put by Dr. Romanes? Why should supernatural design be regarded as possible only if it works suddenly and with a stroke? or why should supernatural design be limited only to special creations? Supposing natural selection true, what is it but another way of indicating design? We are not concerned at present with the ways in which the design argument was once put. It may have been stated inadequately or erroneously, according to the knowledge and ways of thinking at the time. Science has ever claimed the right of restating its theories, the right of making them more general and more consistent with fact. Why should theology be debarred from the same privilege? Science has often stated her case foolishly, and theology may have done so also ; and were we to play at the game of resuscitating past ineptitudes, it is hard to say whether science or theology has most to answer for. Let us admit the doctrine of organic evolution, and we say that Dr. Romanes has supplied us with an argument for design much more magnificent than that based on special creation, the evidence for which he says has been utterly and for ever destroyed. He simply says that the evidence for design is destroyed by that which shows the presence of a vaster design ; for design is all the greater and the more intelligent just in proportion to the complexity of the means and the length of time it takes to bring it about. Professor Huxley puts it thus : " Suppose that any one had been able to show that the watch had not been made directly by any person, but that it was the result of the modification of another watch which kept time but poorly, and that this again had proceeded from a structure which could hardly be called a watch at all, seeing that it had no figures on the dial and the hands were rudimentary, and that, going back and back in time, we come at last to a revolving barrel as the earliest traceable rudiment of the whole fabric ; and imagine that it had been possible to show that all these changes had resulted from a tendency in the structure to vary indefinitely, and, secondly, from something in the surrounding world which helped all variations in the direction of an accurate time-keeper, and checked all those in other directions : then it is obvious that the force of Paley's argument is gone." (*Origin of Species*, Appendix.)

On the contrary, it would appear all the greater, in proportion as a rudimentary watch, which by constant modification could produce other watches, is incomparably more wonderful than any watch made directly by a person. Our friends seem to think that they deny design when they show that the design is greater and more wonderful than human designs ever are. As we ponder on Professor Huxley's illustration, it grows more wonderful under our vision. We have in the rudimentary watch a tendency to vary indefinitely, but that tendency is kept in one direction only by something in the outward world. And Professor Huxley cannot help bringing in teleology, even when he strives with all his might to exclude it. The tendency within controlled by the tendency without, co-ordinated with a view towards the production of "an accurate time-keeper"! Well, a watchmaker constructed the complicated system of wheels, levers, escapement for the same useful end. Thus Professor Huxley could not even state the proposition which denies teleology without the use of language which implied it. All that he has proved is that the intelligence which was needed to produce a watch which evolved other watches was immeasurably greater than that of Paley's watchmaker.

Of many other illustrations I shall refer only to one; and I take it from Professor Lloyd Morgan, whose works on evolution are so valuable and suggestive. "Compare the engines of a modern ocean steamer with even the highest achievement of the age of Watt. Professor Shaw, in his paper on this subject, gives a table to show the number of parts in the engines of a first-class Atlantic liner. In that table we see that no less than twenty-three auxiliary engines minister to the efficiency of the main engine, all being definitely connected together into one complex system. There are no less than thirty-seven separate levers, and a hundred and forty-seven distinct valves, and the total number of parts in the main and auxiliary engines, including nuts, pins, bolts, studs, and so forth, all of them necessary for efficiency, durability, and security, is something like a hundred thousand. . . . Evolution is not the multiplication of similar structures, but the production of one more complex structure which shall do the work of many. Increase of efficiency, increase

6

of complexity, and increase of economy of space, fuel, and material have all gone hand in hand." (*Springs of Conduct*, pp. 159, 160.) The whole section is written with clearness and method, and is graphic and full of interest. We seem to see the evolving of machines. We trace the steam engine step by step, from Watt's somewhat rudimentary engine, till we come to the engine of the Atlantic liner. We are glad to have this illustration of evolution, and we might put it alongside that of Professor Huxley's watch, which was supposed to be able to produce other watches.

It is just possible for us to confine our attention to the series of engines which is brought before us by Professor Lloyd Morgan. We may fix our thought on engine after engine, and admire the successive modifications and their great fitness for the end in view, just as in nature we may fix our thought on the successive modifications of living things from the algæ up to man. We may be so interested in these as to ask no further question, or may look at them as self-explanatory. We may give an explanation of every improvement in the steam engine from the point of view of the engine itself. We may show how each change helped to make it more effective, and we may also show its mechanical fitness. With all this we may leave out of sight the one sufficient explanation of the steam engine. The cause of the engine is the intelligence of the engineer; every step in the evolution was the work of intelligence, working by means and method, and for a foreseen end. All the mechanics of an engine are means to an end, and the engine itself is a means for a still further end, namely, swift and safe communication between people and people, and this end is for yet another end. We have to thank Professor Lloyd Morgan for his illustration. To a system of evolution which involves the same kind of causes, methods, ends as are manifested in the evolution of the steam engine we can have no possible objection. It is just the very kind of evolution we are in search of—an evolution that has reference to a mind that can think and plan and foresee, devise ends, and take means to accomplish the ends in view.

There is no human work which may not be looked at merely in the light of efficient causes as Professor Lloyd Morgan has looked at machines. It is wonderful how much we may explain, without even referring to an inventor or an author. A treatise on a steam engine may not mention the name of Watt from first to last; it may describe the elastic properties of steam, and the laws of expansion and condensation, may deal with the properties of metals, and the forms of cranks, pistons, etc., and speak of all these things just as we speak of the law of gravitation; every part of the engine may thus be explained on mechanical principles, and the work which the engine can do may be calculated exactly to a foot-pound : but we know that the engine had an intelligence as its maker, and a final cause as its end.

In the same way we may study a dialogue of Plato or a play of Shakespeare. Take any working edition of a play of Shakespeare, and we may scarcely have in it a reference to the author. We find notes on philology, which deal in an impersonal way with the history of words and their meaning; we find grammatical expositions, which deal mainly with the laws of grammar; we may find all the resources of human thought and ingenuity tasked to ascertain the meaning of the play. In all these things we are dealing with efficient causes, and we may give a sufficient account of the play from certain points of view without one reference to the author. We may take it as it stands, and seek to understand the law of its becoming, the conditions linguistic, ethical, social which helped to make it what it is; and we may, by an enlightened criticism, ascertain its meaning, and contend plausibly that we have really exhausted the whole matter of the play. Still, there does arise the further question as to the revelation of the author which is in the play, and the fact that the meaning we find in the play was first put into it by a mind like our own. We might run the parallel still more closely. We might point out that each word in the play has its own character and its own particular history determined by law, that each grammatical form of sentence is ruled by logic, and that the connection of part and part may also be closely woven together according to laws which may be formulated; and we may entangle the whole matter in such a complex of laws and necessities as to find no need for a reference to Shakespeare at all.

Now this is exactly parallel to the procedure of those who limit our view of the world to the mere working of efficient causes. We welcome their earnest toil, and we sit at their feet while they unfold for us the wondrous tale of science; we are grateful to them as we are grateful to an expositor of Plato. But when we have learned all that an expositor has to tell us·of the laws of grammar, of philology, of thought, we still have the knowledge that these were plastic in the hands of Plato, and in the end the work is his and his alone. In the same way we may say to our masters in science, after they have taught us all they know about the sequences of things and the laws which govern them : Is this all ? Is this web of life and its laws all you have to tell us ? Have you given us any satisfactory account of the meaning which you have found in the world? You have explained to us the evolution of the steam engine; will you allow us to postulate the same kind of cause for the universe and the same kind of purpose as we know had to do with the evolution of the steam engine ? If not, why not ? Is it b: cause the universe is so much greater than the engine, because the final end is not yet in sight? Well, the answer to that is, to postulate an intelligence equal to the task. The order and adaptation of the universe are as patent as those of the engine ; but if the order and adaptation of the engine are due to intelligence, why make the order and adaptation of the universe a reason for denying that intelligence had to do with the making of it ? Consistency demands that we should assert that the engine evolved itself.

These questions do not arise in connection with the separate sciences. They have enough to do if they deal adequately with their own problems, just as a student will have enough to do if he is to master the principles of construction of the steam engine and the laws and properties of the material employed in its construction. But we should make short work of the contention of that student who asserted that the construction of the engine is altogether due to mechanical causes. The convergence of all these into a system has to be explained. Our contention here is that those who wish to explain the universe from mechanical causes alone are just as rational as the supposed student of the steam engine would be.

The evidence of intelligence is so much greater that our opponents categorically deny it altogether. They may, like Mr. Spencer, say that they deny intelligence in the interests of something greater than intelligence, and then strive as he does, through all the pages of the volumes of the Synthetic Philosophy, to explain the higher in terms of the lower; they may take the order of the universe as an ultimate fact, regarding which no question is to be asked; or they may couch their denial in other terms, and urge it for other reasons. But ultimately the argument seems to come to this : there are so many evidences of intelligence in the universe, that we must therefore infer the absence of a guiding mind.

In truth, the argument from order to intelligence is much more cogent than it was in Paley's time. No one ever strengthened the argument as Darwin has done. Evolution has widened it beyond measure, and the universe, its history and its order, are seen to be worthy of a presiding, guiding intelligence, even of an infinite order. Let us hope that now, when the rapture and the intoxication of the first discovery of evolution have passed away, and sober reflection has come back, that the denial of intelligence to the source and ground of the universe will not be persisted in.

CHAPTER VI

ORGANIC EVOLUTION

Statement by Professor Ray Lankester—New sets of terms used in biology—Why are there new terms ?—Dr. Burdon Sanderson—Darwinism—Variation, struggle for existence, natural selection, transmission—Anthropomorphic character of the process—Malthusianism—Utilitarianism—What is natural selection ?—Comparison with the process of denudation in geology by Mr. J. T. Cunningham—Darwin on the eye—Professor Huxley's reproduction of chance—Organic evolution likely true, but its factors not yet discovered.

THE task which evolution has set itself may be described in the words of Professor E. Ray Lankester : " It is the aim or business of those occupied with biology to assign living things, in all their variety of form and activity, to the one set of forces recognised by the physicist and chemist. Just as the astronomer accounts for the heavenly bodies and their movements by the laws of motion and the property of attraction, as the geologist explains the present state of the earth's crust by the long-continued action of the same forces which at this moment are studied and treated in the form of 'laws' by physicists and chemists ; so the biologist seeks to explain in all its details the long process of the evolution of the innumerable forms of life now existing, or which have

existed in the past, as a necessary outcome, an automatic product, of these same forces." (*Encyc. Brit.*,
vol. xxiv., p. 799*a*.) Again: "It was reserved for
Charles Darwin, in the year 1859, to place the whole
theory of organic evolution on a new footing, and by
his discovery of a mechanical cause actually existing
and demonstrable by which organic evolution must
be brought about to entirely change the attitude in
regard to it of even the most rigid exponents of
the scientific method" (p. 801*b*). "The history of
zoology as a science is therefore the history of the
great doctrine of living things by the natural selection
of varieties in the struggle for existence, since that
doctrine is the one medium whereby all the phenomena
of life, whether of form or function, are rendered
capable of explanation by the laws of physics and
chemistry, and so made the subject-matter of a true
science or study of causes" (p. 799*a*). Professor
Lankester has not explained why in biology he and
those who agree with him have introduced a new set
of terms—terms which are not used in physics or
chemistry. In physics and in chemistry men do not
speak of "advantage," of "utility," of "interest."
But in the article quoted Professor Lankester says:
" Darwin's theory had as one of its results the refor-
mation and the rehabilitation of teleology. According
to that theory, every organ, every part, colour, and
peculiarity of an organism, must either be of benefit
to the organism itself, or have been so to its ancestors;
no peculiarity of structure or general conformation,
no habit or instinct in any organism, can be supposed
to exist for the benefit or amusement of another

organism, not even for the delectation of man himself. Necessarily, according to the theory of natural selection, structures either are present because they are selected as useful, or because they were still inherited from ancestors to whom they were useful, though no longer useful to the existing representatives of these ancestors." (P. 802*b*.)

We know that men, even of the mental stature of Professor Ray Lankester, sometimes do not co-ordinate their notions, or ask whether one part even of a short article is quite consistent with another. If the phenomena of biology have been "rendered capable of explanation by the laws of physics and chemistry," whence this new set of terms unused and unrecognised by these sciences? We do not say in chemistry that any combination must be of benefit either to the molecule or its atoms; nor in mechanics do we speak of "interest," "advantage," "benefit." Do the terms used by Professor Lankester correspond to facts presented by biology? Can the theory of Darwin be even stated without the use of language, which introduces new conceptions not needed by physics or chemistry? Of course every physical body must be consistent with chemical and physical laws; but it is not necessary for us to say that organisms must be capable of explanation by them. If the phenomena of life are to be explained by chemical and physical laws, clearly we are shut out from the use of language implying conceptions which have no place in these sciences. Would it not be well to recognise this, and either refrain from the use of language fitted to mislead, or to admit that there is something in life not to be explained by physical and chemical laws? If we reduce the phenomena of life to physical and chemical laws, they have vanished; if we recognise their distinctive characteristics, then they are no longer explicable by chemical and physical laws.

In his address to the British Association Dr. Burdon Sanderson said : " The methods of investigation being themselves physical or chemical, the organism itself naturally came to be regarded as a complex of such processes and nothing more. In particular the idea of adaptation, which, as I have endeavoured to show, is not a consequence of organism, but its essence, was in a great measure lost sight of." Again : " The specific energy of a part or organ . . . is simply the special action which it normally presents, its norma or rule of action being in each instance the interest of the organism as a whole, of which it forms a part." Could any statement be further removed from the language of physics or chemistry? " The interest of the organism " as a whole gives the norma or rule to each organ; and yet even Dr. Burdon Sanderson says in the same address : " The leading notion was that, however complicated the conditions under which vital energies manifest themselves, they can be split into processes which are identical in nature with those of the non-living world ; and as a corollary to this, that the analysing of a vital process into its physical and chemical constituents, so as to bring these constituents into measurable relations with physical or chemical standards, is the only mode of investigating them which can lead to satisfactory results." The statement is historical, but from the general tenor of the address it would seem to be the view which Dr. Sanderson himself holds. If this be the only method which can lead to satisfactory results, then the task of investigation might well end; for when vital energies are split into processes like those of the non-living world the essential nature of the matter in hand is lost in the splitting.

While the organism in itself does not create energy or matter, yet the transformation of energy and matter in living organisms is quite different from that which takes place in inanimate matter, and to endeavour to explain the one by the other is to lose sight of the initial difference. " The difference between the vitalistic and mechanical schools might indeed be regarded as one of words; it is, however, one of ideas. As one of the speakers said, the tendency of the official physiology of the text-book and the laboratory, the lecture-room and the examination-hall, has been to narrow its field to the investigation that requires the precise instruments of physics and chemistry, and to ignore the fruitful field now successfully tilled by the zoologist and the botanist, whose results are expressible only in the terminology of intelligent speech, not in grains, centimeters, seconds, or degrees. This is the cause of the aridity of so much modern physiology, almost divorced from the study of protoplasmic life, of experimental embryology, and of heredity." (Marcus Hartog, in *Speaker*, Sept. 3rd, 1893.) The truth of the charge brought by Mr. Hartog is very evident, and this comparative barrenness is due to the belief held by many, and formulated by Professor Ray

Lankester, that the laws of chemistry and physics are capable of explaining the phenomena of life. But when the ideas of struggle, of advantage, of vitality, and other ideas of the same order enter in, we have passed from mechanics, and have entered a sphere wherein new phenomena reign, and these phenomena have laws peculiar to themselves. They may use the powers of chemistry and physics, but they use them in their own way and for new ends and purposes.

But we may try to obtain a real view of what Mr. Darwin has done, and seek to understand what natural selection is, and does, and can do. It is not necessary for us to trace the history of this great conception, or to dwell on the fact that there were evolutionists before Darwin. Such histories there are in abundance : for example, in the articles on " Evolution " by Professor Huxley and Professor Sully, in the latest edition of the *Encyclopædia Britannica*. Darwin and Wallace, however, turned an abstract speculation into a working hypothesis. They were able to show how evolution might be brought about. They were able to point to causes actually at work in the play of organic life around us, and that if similar causes were at work for a long period back then the web of life might be understood and explained. As stated by Mr. A. R. Wallace the great principles of Darwinism are these. Two main classes of facts are apparent to us when we look at life and its manifestations. The first is the enormous increase of organisms. They tend to increase in geometrical progression, while their means of subsistence tend to increase in arithmetical progression. Hence there must be a struggle for existence, for the number of the offspring greatly exceeds the number of the parents. They compete with each other, they are destroyed also by cold and heat, rain and snow, floods and storm. "There is thus a perpetual struggle among them which shall live and which shall die ; and this struggle is tremendously severe, because so few can possibly remain alive" (*Darwinism*, p. 11). Along with the struggle there is a second class of facts, which is summed up under the names of variation and transmission. There are variations, for all individuals of a species are not alike ; if they were alike, there would be no grounds for the survival of one rather than another. But individuals do vary, and vary in many ways. Some may be stronger, swifter, more healthy, more cunning, may have a colour which gives them a better chance of hiding, may have keener sight, and any beneficial variation will help the individual in the struggle, and the fittest will be sure to survive.

Beneficial variations will be transmitted from one generation to another, and the effect will be cumulative. Natural selection will secure that the variation best suited to its environment will survive ; and as the action of natural selection is constant, new variations will be selected ; and thus, in each generation, the fittest will survive, and so long as the variations are beneficial they will go on and will accumulate. Natural selection, acting on variations which somehow arise, accumulating the variations and transmitting them from generation to generation, is held to account for the origin and survival of all the organic species now in existence on the earth.

Now it would be idle to deny the great merit of Darwin's work, or the reality of the process which he describes. Organisms are produced in such abundance that it is impossible they can all survive. Some of the plants and animals which are constantly being produced must perish, and those perish which are least adapted and those survive which are best adapted to the conditions of existence. Natural selection is just the process by which the fittest are picked out and the least fit are left to perish.

So far all is clear and intelligible. But it is interesting to notice how much of ourselves and our nature we have thus read into nature. We have indeed, under the guidance of Darwin and Wallace, explained nature in terms of human nature. We do not object ; for man is always the middle term in our interpretation of the world. We expect nature to be rational, to respond to our intelligence and to our methods, and we find the correspondence does exist and is real. We do, however, object to the constant denunciation of anthropomorphism by men who are the most anthropomorphic of any. The term natural selection is in Darwin's own words : " This preservation of favourable differences and variations, and the destruction of those which are injurious, I have called natural selection, or the survival of the fittest." The term itself is borrowed from that progressive selection practised by man in the rearing of domesticated animals and cultivated plants. Slight differences may be accumulated in one direction during many generations until what looks like a new species is produced. " The key," says Darwin, " is man's

power of accumulative selection; nature gives successive variations; man adds them up in certain directions
useful to him." This kind of language is readily
understood, and every one may at once see what is
meant. It seems that the variations are already
given, and man selects those varieties which tend in
a certain direction, and leaves them free to breed
together. The breeder takes advantage of the tendency to variation, and also of the tendency to the
accumulation of variations; but he is unable to
explain the variation or the accumulation. It is to
be observed also that, so far as the action of the
breeder is concerned, we have had recourse to a
selecting agency beyond the organism itself. The
purpose is in the mind of the breeder, and not in
the organism or the environment.

What the breeder effects by conscious selection,
the struggle for existence is supposed to effect in
organic beings in a state of nature. Man selects
what is useful to man; Nature selects what is for
the good of the individual or the species, in the
competition with rivals. It is difficult to pass from
man's conscious selection to natural selection; if we
do, however, let us observe in passing how anthropomorphic we are. We may acknowledge that the
process is similar in both cases. Looking away for
the moment from man's selecting care, we observe
that the process consists in leaving those forms
which have certain peculiarities free to breed together. Other forms are removed by the agency of
the breeder. But there is also a selective breeding
due to the killing out of competing forms by the

struggle for existence. "As man," says Darwin, "can produce a great result with his domestic animals and plants by adding up in any given direction individual differences, so could natural selection, but far more easily from having incomparably longer time for action." We note in passing the likening of nature's work to man's, and we also note that results are ascribed both to nature's work and to man's, which they are not competent to produce. Darwin admits that man "can neither originate varieties nor prevent their occurrence." "He can only preserve and accumulate such as do occur." He assumes that man can accumulate, and proceeds to assume that natural selection can also accumulate. "It may metaphorically be said that natural selection is daily and hourly scrutinising throughout the world the slightest variations, rejecting those that are bad and adding up all that is good." Yes; but in the sequel we pass from the metaphor, and we are made to believe that we have referred the origin of species to purely natural causation. When we examine the metaphor somewhat closely, we find that all we have got from Mr. Darwin is this : beings with the most serviceable variations survive in the struggle for existence.

Professor Huxley, in his animated and interesting paper contributed to the *Life of Darwin*, says: "The suggestion that new species may result from the selective action of external conditions upon the variations from their specific type which individuals present —and which we call 'spontaneous' because we are ignorant of their causation—is as wholly unknown to

7

the historian of scientific ideas as it was to biological specialists before 1858. But that suggestion is the central idea of the *Origin of Species*, and contains the quintessence of Darwinism." (Vol. ii., p. 195.) " That which we were looking for and could not find was a hypothesis respecting the origin of known organic forms, which assumed the operation of no causes but such as could be proved to be actually at work. We wanted not to pin our faith to that or any other speculation, but to get hold of clear and definite conceptions which could be brought face to face with facts, and have their validity tested. The *Origin* provided us with the working hypothesis we wanted. Moreover, it did the immense service of freeing us for ever from the dilemma, Refuse to accept the creation hypothesis, and what have you to propose that can be accepted by any cautious reasoner? In 1857 I had no answer ready, and I do not think that any one else had. A year later we reproached ourselves with dulness for being perplexed by such an inquiry. My reflection, when I first made myself master of the central idea of the *Origin*, was ' How extremely stupid not to have thought of that.' . . . The facts of variability, of the struggle for existence, of adaptation to conditions were notorious enough ; but none of us had suspected that the road to the heart of the species problem lay through them, until Darwin and Wallace dispelled the darkness, and the beacon-fire of the *Origin* guided the benighted." (P. 197.)

The Professor is enthusiastic, and we do not wonder. He had " got hold of clear and definite conceptions

which could be brought face to face with facts."
The conceptions, as we have seen, are not quite clear.
The appropriate machinery was largely metaphorical ;
the struggle for existence was exaggerated. If we
want to have any principle of science or philosophy
pushed to an extreme, we always have recourse to
Mr. Grant Allen. "The baker does not fear the
competition of the butcher in the struggle for life ; it
is the competition of other bakers that sometimes
inexorably crushes him out of existence. . . . In this
way the great enemies of the individual herbivores
are not the carnivores, but the other herbivores. . . .
It is not so much the battle between the tiger and
the antelope, between the wolf and the bison, between
the snake and the bird, that ultimately results in
natural selection or survival of the fittest, as the
struggle between tiger and tiger, between bison and
bison, between snake and snake, between antelope and
antelope." (Quoted in *The Study of Animal Life*, by
J. Arthur Thomson, p. 38.) Thus Mr. Grant Allen, in
his anthropomorphic way, takes the struggle between
baker and baker, and makes it the typical struggle of
the universe. And the same may be said of natural
selection. So also we might see the extension of the
human analogy in the large part which " utility " has
played in the Darwinian theory. "Any being, if it
vary, however slightly, in any manner profitable to
itself, will have a better chance of surviving, and thus
be naturally selected." Every structure either now
is or was formerly of some direct or indirect use
to its possessor. In fact, natural selection rests on
" utility," and this is nothing else than the extension

to the organic world of the national utilitarian ethics.

Malthusianism and utilitarianism are main elements in the theory of Darwin. The principle of utility, however, does not seem to have any relation to the origin of species. The selection of the useful in the struggle for existence does not explain the origin of new characters. Utility is after all only a relative conception, and it cannot possibly be the fundamental principle of the organic world. Utility is an attribute of what is; a character or quality must first exist before it can be useful. It has no utility before it existed, and it can have none during the period of its formation. Utility leaves untouched the question of the means by which it has been brought into existence. " Selection, whether natural or artificial, is perfectly analogous to the process of denudation in geology. It explains the extinction of innumerable forms, and the consequent gaps and intervals which separate species, families, orders, etc.; just as denudation explains the want of continuity in the stratified rocks. But geologists have never been blind enough to suppose that the evolution of the structure of a given rock was due to denudation; they have always believed that the structure of each rock was due to the effects of the forces which have acted upon it since its formation, and they have devoted their energies to tracing by observation and experiment the effects of the various forces." (Preface to Eimer's *Organic Evolution*, by J. T. Cunningham, p. xxi.)

With this view of the action of natural selection Mr. Darwin seems himself to agree : " Several writers have misapprehended or objected to the term 'natural selection'; some have even imagined that natural selection **induces variability**, whereas it implies only the preservation of such variations as arise and are beneficial to the being under its conditions of life" (*Origin of Species*, p. 110). But does Mr. Darwin himself always use the words in this sense? On the contrary, we find that he constantly speaks of natural selection as able to " produce structures." Take his description of the evolution of the eye : " When we reflect on these facts, here given much too briefly, with respect to the wide, diversified, and graduated range of structure in the eyes of the lower animals; and when we bear in mind how small the number of all living forms must be in comparison with those which have become extinct, the difficulty ceases to be very great in believing that natural selection may have converted the simple apparatus of an optic nerve coated with pigment and invested by transparent membrane into an optical instrument as perfect as possessed by any member of the Articulate Class" (sect. 275). Further on there is a marvellous passage : " If we must compare the eye to an optical instrument, we ought in imagination to take a thick layer of transparent tissue, with spaces filled with fluid, and with a nerve sensitive to light beneath, and then suppose every part of this layer to be continually changing slowly in density, so as to separate into layers of different densities and thicknesses, placed at different distances from each other, and with the surface of each layer slowly changing in form. Further, we must suppose that there is a power, represented by natural selection or the survival of the fittest, always intently watching each slight alteration in the transparent layers; and carefully preserving each which, under varied circumstances, in any way, or in any degree, tends to produce a distincter image. We must suppose each new state of the instrument to be multiplied by the million, each to be preserved until a better one is produced, and then the old ones to be all destroyed. In living bodies variation will cause the slight alterations, generation will multiply them almost infinitely, and natural selection will pick out with unerring skill each improvement. Let this process go on for millions of years, and during each year on millions of individuals of many kinds; and may we not believe that a living optical instrument might thus be formed, as superior to one of glass as the works of the Creator are to those of man?" (Sect. 277.) "Reason tells me that, if numerous gradations, from a simpler and imperfect eye to one complex and perfect, can be shown to exist, each grade being useful to its possessor, as is certainly the case; if, further, the eye ever varies, and the variations be inherited, as is likewise certainly the case; and if such variations should be useful to the animal under changing conditions of life, then the difficulty of believing that a perfect and complex eye could be formed by natural selection, though insuperable to our imagination, should not be considered as subversive of the theory" (sect. 271). "Formed by natural selection," "natural selection always intently watching each slight alteration," "natural selection will pick out with unerring skill each improvement." Truly the functions performed by Natural Selection are great ! At one time it watches, then **it picks** out, then it accumulates, and lastly it has a " productive " power. At one time Darwin claims nothing for it but the power of eliminating the least advantageous eyes, and suddenly this claim changes into a claim to produce advantageous eyes. But though natural selection may explain how a particular eye came to be preserved, it tells us nothing of the formation of any eye.

We are not concerned to deny the theory of organic evolution, nor even to say that Darwin's account of the evolution of the eye is improbable. What we are concerned with is the bearing of his theory on teleology. And we see that his view is not in-compatible with design. He cannot dispense with superintendence, nor with an agency which watches, picks out, accumulates, and forms. The question is, To whom or to what shall we ascribe this selecting power ? To foresight, to forethought, or to what ? One does not care to ascribe to learned and thoughtful men views which they have earnestly repudiated. They have denied most emphatically that they believe in " chance " as a cause. They use the word because they do not know the causes of variation. Still, they use the word, and they use it not only as a name for the action of causes which they do not know, but they use it as if it produced something. Variation is fortuitous. Variations are in all directions, and those which happened to hit on a stable combination survived· But this is chance. Variations, however, are not indefinite. If variations are in definite directions, if

" a whale does not tend to vary in the direction of
producing feathers, nor a bird in the direction of producing whalebone," then manifestly natural selection is
not incompatible with design.   May we not say that
natural selection is design?   It may, indeed, be said
that, though variation now proceeds in definite lines,
or in certain fixed directions, it was not always so.
There may have been a time when life proceeded
indefinitely in all directions, and reached positions
of temporary stable equilibrium only after a series of
trials and errors.   But that is a mere speculation,
and is not worthy of the name of science.   Life has
had a certain bent from the beginning of life; it
has proceeded along certain lines, and has grown in
certain directions, and the bent and set are just the
very things to be accounted for.

The issue to-day is, we repeat, not between " evolution " and what our friends are pleased to call
" special creation."   It is between evolution under the
guidance of intelligence and purpose, and evolution
as a fortuitous result.   " According to teleology, each
organism is like a rifle bullet fired straight at a mark;
according to Darwin organisms are like grape shot, of
which one hits something and the rest fall wide.
For the teleologist an organism exists for the conditions in which it was found; for the Darwinian an
organism exists, because out of many of its kind it
is the only one which has been able to persist in the
conditions in which it was found."   (Huxley, *On the
Origin of Species*, Appendix.)   We do not accept
this account of teleology; nor do we know whence
Professor Huxley derived the notion.   At all events,

what teleology demands is that we do recognise those adaptations to purpose which are so manifest in the universe, of which also the works of Darwin are so full. It is not necessary to teleology to suppose that "each organism is fired straight at a mark." What is necessary is that the organism hits the mark. If the hitting of the mark is accomplished by a persistent process prolonged throughout the centuries, implying completeness of arrangement and adjustment of means to ends in a complicated series, then the result is not against teleology; on the contrary, it simply heightens our view of the skill of the teleologist.

If we can in a measure understand the steps of the process and the magnitude of the operation, as Darwin and Huxley enable us to do, then our wonder is made all the greater, and we fall prostrate before the unutterable wisdom of the intelligence which made the world. Such a teleology is not opposed to evolution; but it is opposed to Professor Huxley's "grape-shot" view of the universe. Yet in his article in the *Life of Darwin* Professor Huxley is indignant with those who "charge Mr. Darwin with having attempted to reinstate the old pagan goddess Chance"; and he adds: "Probably the best answer to those who talk of Darwinism meaning the reign of 'Chance' is to ask them what they themselves mean by 'chance.' Do they believe that anything in this universe happens without reason and without a cause? Do they really conceive that any event has no cause, or could not have been predicted by any one who had a sufficient insight into the order of nature?" (*Life of Darwin,* pp. 200, 201.) Really Professor Huxley, by his description of Darwinism as a "method of trial and error" and of organisms as being like "grape shot of which one hits something and the rest fall wide," has done more than anybody else to fasten the charge on Mr. Darwin of having attempted to reinstate the old pagan goddess Chance. He should restrain his indignation. How does his grape-shot illustration agree with "the one act of faith in the convert to science," namely, "the confession of the universality of order, and of the absolute validity in all times and under all circumstances of the law of causation"? Where is the causation in the organism which hits and the organisms which fall wide? Could any one, however great his insight into the order of nature, have predicted which one would hit and which would fall wide? Why should any organism hit anything in the circumstances? Need we wonder that any one, having read Professor Huxley on the origin of species, should come to the conclusion that the essence of Darwinism was just this appeal to chance? The appeal to "lucky accidents" is made so often by Mr. Darwin and his followers that one can hardly help thinking of the "lucky accident" as having a part to play in the constitution of things.

Leaving chance and accident out of account on both sides, our contention is that teleology gives us the only tenable explanation of the history of life on the earth. The evidence of organic evolution is so vast, so varied, that most people nowadays must accept the conclusion to which it points. Naturalists are convinced that the plants and animals of to-day are descended from others of a simpler sort, and that these are descended from others yet more simple, and thus we may conceivably go back to the first beginnings of life. The arguments of Darwin are based on the distribution of animals in space, their successive appearance in time, on actual variations in domestication, cultivation, and in nature, on facts of structure, and on embryology. The evidence seems irresistible. Most scientific men accept it ; and they have their rights, and are bound to uphold, vindicate, and expound what they believe to be true. If organic evolution, then, be accepted as true, where do we stand ? Have we any interest in what is called " special creations " ? If we believe in intelligence as the cause of order, then we should expect that all organic forms have arisen in conformity with uniform laws, and not through breaches of uniform law. We no longer believe—whatever men did once believe—that plants and animals were suddenly thrust into the complex conditions of their life ; that the complex of inner relations was suddenly and in a moment adjusted to the complex of outer relations ; or that the actual concrete life of a plant or an animal was thus originated and perpetuated. But creation by evolution is still creation.

Evolution is opposed only to a particular theory of creation, and that theory was as much scientific as religious. There is a theory of special creation which can be no longer held. The view was that each species or kind was directly created by God at the beginning of the world, and has gone on reproducing itself after its kind. The clearest statement of this view is to be

found in the great botanist Linnæus, who held that
" there are just so many species as there are different
forms created by the infinite Being; and these
different forms, according to the laws of reproduction
imposed on them, produced others, but always forms
like themselves." We have something like the same
view in Milton's *Paradise Lost* : lions, tigers, stags, all
ready-made, working their way out of the earth,—

> " The tawny lion, pawing to get free
> His hinder parts," etc.

At the beginning of this century the belief was
universal, both among religious and scientific men, that
species were fixed and never passed into each other.
Now all this is altered, and most scientific men hold a
doctrine of descent, or evolution.

It is clear that the doctrine of special creation as
set forth, say, by Linnæus, is inconsistent with the
doctrine of Darwin. And if organic evolution is true,
we have to ask, Are we committed to the doctrine
of special creation? or rather, Is the doctrine of
special creation as above defined an essential part
of theism or Christianity? There was a time when
men earnestly contended for the immutability of
species, and thought that important consequences
would follow from the denial of it. But that time
is past, and the immutability of species happily
forms no part of the creed of Christendom nor of the
teaching of Scripture; for the creeds of Christendom
simply affirm that God is the Maker of the world and
all that is in it, and does not say anything about
the way and manner in which He made them. The

Scripture says that " He maketh the grass to grow on the mountains "; but says nothing about whether He caused it to grow suddenly or otherwise, directly or indirectly. The Scriptures teach a doctrine of descent, and have no hesitation in saying that all the races of men are descended from one father, and " God hath made of one blood all the nations of the earth." If all the races of men are modified descendants of one primeval man, and if descent with modification can account for all of them, where is the objection on Scriptural and theological grounds to accepting a theory which simply extends to the whole world of organic life a principle which theology has always contended for as true with respect to man? Theology has had its difficulties with regard to Traducianism and Creationism; and the same difficulties, and no greater, appear with respect to evolution and special creation. What is essential is that we maintain and vindicate the continued dependence of all creation on its Maker, and that if things are made so as to make themselves, God is their Maker after all; and if evolution can tell us anything of the method of creation and the order in which the different forms of life appeared, then we ought to rejoice in it.

CHAPTER VII

ORGANIC EVOLUTION (Continued)

Biology before and after Darwin—Physical continuity of life
—Laws and conditions of life—Adequacy or inadequacy
of Natural Selection?—Inter-relations of life—Professor
Geddes on anthropomorphism of the nineteenth century
and of the eighteenth—Weismann—Natural selection is
elimination of the unfit—Oscillation between natural
selection as negative and as positive—Poulton, "that
selection is examination"—Teleology run mad—Mimicry
—Search after utility—Mutual benefit of species in
co-operation—Illustration—Struggle for existence thus
modified—Results.

THE contrast between works on biology which
were written before the appearance of Darwin's
Origin of Species and those which have appeared
since that great work is most striking. There can
be no doubt that biologists have got hold of a most
fruitful hypothesis, and the conceptions introduced
by Darwin have shed a great light on the sciences
which deal with life. Things which seemed to be far
apart and isolated from one another have suddenly
been seen to be closely connected, and structures and
organisms are seen to be related to one another, and
to be parts of an intelligible whole. The full and
adequate appreciation of the worth of the facts
and of the laws can be grasped completely only by

those who are specially qualified; but one who is not a specialist may apprehend the breadth and grandeur of the conception which enables him to think of all life as a unity and to trace the innumerable living forms to slow variation from a single stock. This conception leaves the mystery of life where it found it: origins lie beyond the action of this conception. Science tells us that life comes from life, and it is powerless to explain the origin of life. Let life be given, and science says it can trace its path of progress, and understand some of the laws which have guided its development. Clearly, then, we must give heed to the statements of science, and endeavour to apprehend their meaning. If all living forms are to be traced back to some simple organism, and if there is a physical continuity of life, what attitude are we to assume with regard to this claim? What is its theological significance? Has it any more significance for theology than the claim which theology was wont to make, and which science sometimes seemed to deny, namely, that all the varieties of the human family are descended from one pair? If we can say that mankind is one without falling into theological ineptitude, why may we not admit that all life is one, and has grown from the one simple form to the varied forms which now teem upon the earth? If the Negro and the Englishman are varieties of one stock, why not also the vertebrate and the invertebrate?

It is difficult indeed to imagine the course of development, and difficult also to imagine the forces which brought it about. Still, those who know the subject and have studied it most thoroughly tell us, with growing confidence, that the growth of species by a process of slow development is an established fact.   They are entitled to speak ; and the evidence they produce is of the highest order, and we may rest assured that questions of biology will be settled by biology, on scientific grounds, and on these alone. It seems a reasonable claim so far.   It claims not that it can show how life originated, but that, given life, it has developed according to certain laws, and that these laws have so far been discovered.   There does not seem to be anything here to which we can object.   That life has proceeded according to law is as reasonable as is the supposition that the solar system is ruled by law.   The recognition of any law in nature implies that law rules everywhere.

While there is agreement among the masters as to the general doctrine of evolution that all the forms of life have been evolved from some simpler form of life, there is a wide difference of opinion as to what the factors of evolution are.   All are agreed as to the weaving of the web of life, but by no means are they agreed as to the factors or the agents by which the web is woven.   Some, of whom Russel Wallace may be taken as the chief and the greatest, believe in the adequacy of natural selection, and would shut out all other agencies whatever.   Sexual selection, physiological selection he explains by means of natural selection.   On the other hand, Herbert Spencer writes on the " Inadequacy of Natural Selection," and lays great stress on other " factors of evolution."   Darwin himself said in 1876 : " In my

opinion the greatest error which I have committed
has been not allowing sufficient weight to the direct
action of the environment, *i.e.*, food, climate, etc.,
independently of natural selection" (*Life*, vol. iii.,
p. 159). And Mr. Spencer has always laid great
stress on the direct action of the environment.
Almost all are agreed as to the fact of evolution;
but there is a wide difference as to the factors in
the process. It is still an open question what are
the primary factors in evolution; but whether stress
is laid on the organism itself, or on its function, or
on the environment, there need be no hesitation in
saying how great is the process, and how wide an
outlook it has given us over the whole field of life.
It is no longer possible for us to think of things and
of life in the old fixed static way. The adaptations,
the inter-relations, the incessant movement of life
revealed to us under the guidance of biologists are
simply marvellous. We may not yet know fully how
these adaptations and inter-relations are brought
about, but the fact of their existence is undoubted.
The world is much more wonderful than we know.
What can be more wonderful than the relation of
the insect to the flower, or the successive steps by
which they have wrought out their mutual form and
destiny? What more wonderful than the part which
is played in the world of nature by these invisible
germs, which at some times are destructive of the
more developed life, and at other times are indispensable to its continuance? It would appear that without the help of bacteria wheat could not be grown.
All the forms of life seem, indeed, to be related to each

other by innumerable ties, and the inter-relations are simply more marvellous than up to the present time have been suspected by man.

At the same time, we are not quite sure that we have yet got into the sphere of pure science when we have substituted Darwin for Paley. We have got into a larger world, a world of more complex relations; but are we not still in the world of anthropomorphism? To quote Professor Geddes, one of the most profound thinkers of our time, and one whose scientific work is of the highest value: "Taking a larger instance, the substitution of Darwin for Paley as the chief interpreter of the order of nature is currently regarded as the displacement of an anthropomorphic view for a purely scientific one. A little reflection will show that what has actually happened has been merely the replacement of the anthropomorphism of the eighteenth century for the anthropomorphism of the nineteenth. For the place vacated by the logical and metaphysical explanation has simply been occupied by that suggested to Darwin and Wallace by Malthus in terms of the prevalent severity of industrial competition, and those phenomena of struggle for existence which the light of contemporary economic theory has enabled us to discern, have thus come to be temporarily exalted into a complete explanation of the organic process." (*Chambers' Encyclopædia*, art. "Biology.") Professor Geddes believes in evolution, but does not believe in the struggle for existence and natural selection as primary factors of the process. For myself I have tried to read with an open mind what has been written on natural selection and I have not been able to see that the writers in question have succeeded in using the phrase in a consistent manner. Darwin and Wallace have, in fact, left the problem of the origin of variation alone, and have given their strength to the establishing of the theory of the origin of species by means of natural selection. It is obvious, however, that we have not even approached the question of the origin of species until we have some definite notion of the causes of variation. Indefinite variation affords no solution, and the action of natural selection can, as has frequently been observed, produce nothing.

Perhaps the best illustration of the way in which evolutionists pass unconsciously from the destructive and eliminative action of natural selection to something which may be looked at as positive, constructive, and productive may be found in the language of Weismann : " To state my meaning more clearly, Charles Darwin and Alfred Russel Wallace have taught us to understand by ' natural selection ' that process of elimination effected by nature itself without the aid of man. Inasmuch as far more individuals are born than can possibly live, only the best are fitted to survive, the best being those which are so formed as to be the ' fittest,' as we say, for the conditions of life in which they are placed. As in each generation only the fittest survive and propagate the species, their qualities only are transmitted, while the less useful qualities of the weaker individuals die out. Each successive generation will therefore consist of individuals better organised than those of the preceding one, and thus useful characters will be gradually intensified from generation to generation, until the greatest possible degree of perfection is reached. Probably this theory is far from new to many of my readers. It has been so often explained in various well-known works and periodicals that any further elucidation is unnecessary. What holds good for the individual as a whole, also holds good for each separate organ, inasmuch as the ability of an animal to perform its allotted function depends on the efficiency of each particular organ : hence by means of the perpetual elimination of the unfit every organ is brought to the highest perfection. On this hypothesis, and on this only, is it possible to explain the wonderful adaptability of the minutest details of structure in animals and plants and the development of the organic world through the operation of natural forces. If this view be the true one, if adaptation in all the parts of living forms be truly the result of natural selection, then the same process which produced these adaptations will tend to preserve them, and they will disappear directly natural selection ceases to act." (Weismann on *Heredity*, vol. ii., p. 16, English translation.)

Weismann has formerly defined natural selection as a " process of elimination "; that is to say, a process which is destructive and negative. Immediately it changes in his hands into a process which is constructive and positive. Let us substitute the definition of natural selection in the last sentence for natural selection itself, and see how it reads. " If adaptation in all its parts be the result of a ' process of elimination,' then the same process which produced these results will tend to preserve them, and they will disappear directly the 'process of elimination' has ceased to work." It now reads like nonsense. There is surely something fallacious in a process of reasoning which defines a term and then changes the definition in the course of a single paragraph.

Nor is this procedure peculiar to Weismann. It is constantly being used by Russel Wallace, and by the pure Darwinians of every shade. "Natural selection has already pronounced a satisfactory verdict upon the vast majority of animals which have reached maturity. The male which has only just passed this test, and is nevertheless accepted because of some superior attraction, will soon succumb, and will leave far less offspring than one of equal or perhaps inferior attractions which is fitted to live for the natural term of his life. Natural Selection is a qualifying examination, which must be passed by all candidates for honours ; Sexual Selection is an honours examination, in which many who have passed the previous examination will be rejected." (*The Colour of Animals*, by Edward Bagnall Poulton, p. 308.) We accept Mr. Poulton's metaphor, and we wish that he had used natural selection in this sense throughout. To examine, however, is a different function from production, and throughout his book he speaks of natural selection not as examining but as preparing candidates for examination. But we believe that neither in Oxford nor in nature need the examiner and the trainer be the same person. The examination reveals the fitness, it does not make it ; and yet Mr. Poulton continually speaks as if the examination had prepared and made the candidate who succeeds in passing it.   There are universities which do not teach, they only examine; they simply test the knowledge of candidates, and leave them to obtain that knowledge where they like.   But they have no claim to have made the fitness; they simply say that the candidate is fit.   It would be well if the phrase " natural selection " were used in a consistent manner, and were limited to the process of elimination of the " unfit."   As it is used it simply misleads, and causes us to think that we have a true productive cause when as a matter of fact we have none.

This double meaning of the phrase has also other consequences theoretical and practical. For one thing, it has set men to seek for possible advantages which may accrue to the organism by any slight organic modification.   The literature of Darwinism abounds with such processes of search and discovery.   It looks sometimes as if here we had a teleology run mad. No Bridgewater treatise is so teleological as almost any Darwinian book we may happen to open.   One enthusiastic disciple of the older teleology is said to have remarked that it was striking that all the large rivers ran near large cities, and on the assumption that the large towns were there first made many wise reflections.   The modern teleology has many remarks quite as wise and as relevant. We have, for example, the following from Mr. Poulton: " A very beautiful and familiar illustration (of recognition markings in animals) is given by Mr. Wallace—the white, upturned tail of the rabbit, by which the young and inexperienced or the least wary individuals are shown the way to the burrow. . . . The tail of the rabbit only becomes conspicuous when it is needed by other individuals of the same species, and when the animal is already alarmed and in full retreat for a place of security." (*Colour of Animals*, p. 212.) Another interpretation quite as plausible, though lacking in the conspicuous element of utility to the rabbit, is that the tail of the rabbit is of great advantage to the dog who pursues it, for it directs his path straight to the mark ; or to the sportsman, who knows at once where to shoot. In these instances the possession of a white tail is of disadvantage to the rabbit.

As we turn over the pages of Mr. Poulton's most interesting book, we are filled with admiration of the wisdom, insight, and foresight of the creatures whose colouring he describes. " I know," he says, " of no more inspiring subject than the colour of birds' eggs. The most superficial glance over a collection of eggs reveals hosts of interesting problems which require solution. I look forward to the time when any description of colour and marking will be considered incomplete unless supplemented by an account of their meaning and importance in the life of the species." (Pp. 66, 67.) The assumption is that every shade of colour and every form of marking have a meaning, and are of importance towards the life of the species. On this assumption Mr. Wallace and Mr. Poulton have proceeded, and have made their illustrations. Thus colours are of direct physiological value, or they give protective or aggressive resemblance, or they have protective and aggressive mimicry, or they give warning, or they have a significance of beauty in courtship.

Thus the colours of animals are always significant, whatever that significance may be. Speaking of mimicry, Mr. Poulton says : " It not only supported the doctrine of evolution, but it afforded strong confirmation of the theory of natural selection, by which Darwin explained how it was that evolution took place. Every step in the gradually increasing change of the mimicking in the direction of specially protected form would have an advantage in the struggle for existence, while the elements out of which the resemblance was built exist in the individual variability of the species, a variability which is hereditary." (P. 220.) Here is the Darwinian theory in a nutshell, with all its plausibility and with all its difficulty. The causes which produced the gradual mimicking are not in the organism, nor in the environment, nor even in the relations between organism and environment. Mr. Poulton quotes the following from Mr. Skertchly, and describes it as extraordinary. This theory "presupposes (*a*) that danger is universal; (*b*) that some butterflies escape danger by secreting a nauseous fluid ; (*c*) that other butterflies noticed this immunity ; (*d*) that they copied it." His own view is that " the mimicry alluded to in these pages is of course unconscious, and has been gradually produced by the operation of natural selection." What is it, then, which produces mimicry ? We can learn from Mr. Poulton that mimicry is useful when it has been produced. He himself says that the volition of an animal could not account for all the details of mimetic resemblance. Still, Mr. Poulton sometimes speaks as if the volition of the animal meant something in the process : "Such caterpillars terrify their enemies by the suggestion of a cobra-like serpent ; for the head of a snake is not large, while its eyes are small and not specially conspicuous. The cobra, however, inspires alarm by the large eye-like 'spectacles' upon the dilated hood, and thus offers an appropriate model for the swollen anterior end of the caterpillar with its terrifying markings." (P. 259.) The mode of speech is peculiar. May we venture to ask about the "model" and its "appropriateness"? To whom or to what does the model sit, and by what means is it imitated? If we shut out the volition of the animal, what have we left? It may be answered that the language used is metaphorical, descriptive, pictorial. But the answer is that we have already had too much of the metaphorical in this department of science, and the theory of natural selection has taken full advantage of what is merely metaphorical. It has grown to be a kind of *deus ex machina*, which seems to preside over all changes of organisms, and which, belonging neither to the organism nor its environment, but being in a manner above both, gives to the evolutionist all the advantages of a presiding intelligence without its disadvantages. Natural selection is itself described as a metaphor; but as soon as we begin to work with it its metaphorical character disappears, and it becomes intensely real, and is quite capable of doing anything. It has the character constantly ascribed to it both of a directing agency and of a presiding intelligence; and it does seem as if both were needed if evolution is to be an intelligible process. "May not," asks

Mr. Arthur Thomson, "the similar surroundings and habits of mimickers and mimicked have sometimes something to do with their resemblance? may it not be that the presence of the mimicked has had a direct, but of course very subtle, influence on the mimickers? is it altogether absurd to suppose that there may be an element of consciousness in the resemblance between oriole and friar-bird?" (*The Study of Animal Life*, p. 61.) Evidently to explain the colours of animals we need something more than the action of natural selection upon casual changes.

Mr. Poulton describes well the number of ways in which the puss moth defends itself. It resembles the leaves of the willow and poplar, on which it feeds. When disturbed it assumes a terrifying attitude mimetic of a vertebrate appearance. The effect is heightened by two pink whips which are swiftly protruded from the prongs of the fork in which the body terminates; it can also eject an irritant fluid. And yet, with all these combined means of defence, it fails to defend itself. " Any improvement in the means of defence has been met by the greater ingenuity or boldness of foes; and so it has come about that many of the best-protected larvæ are often those which die in the largest numbers from the attacks of enemies. The exceptional standard of defence has been reached only by the pressure of an exceptional need." (*Colour of Animals*, pp. 277, 278.) The last sentence is unexpected. If the well-protected larvæ are often those which die in the largest numbers from the attacks of enemies, we should have expected Mr. Poulton to have congratulated the victor on the success of the attack, and not the vanquished on the failure of its attempts at protection.

The conflict here depicted reminds one of the race between the builders of armoured vessels and the manufacturers of guns. The heavier armour was met by the production of larger, more powerful guns ; and it is now found that any armour that a ship can carry may be penetrated by an Armstrong or a Krupp gun. The limit of defence has been found on that line. The conflict between defence and attack receives an illustration from the work of Professor Stahl on the conflict between snails and plants. He shows that plants save themselves from being eaten by snails in fifteen different kinds of ways, and he interprets these various kinds of protection as if they had been produced in order to protect the plants from snails. Plants which were sweet were eaten, and a plant that happened to be sour escaped. Natural selection preserved the sour plant and propagated it; and, as Professor Geddes says, vegetation tends to grow sourer to all eternity. " To give snails credit for evolving plants with crystals, sourness, and poison, to make cattle and the like responsible for the thorns on plants, is like giving snakes the credit of evolving boots which protect our heels. In all these cases alike the possibility of some defensive utility is undenied, nor even of some improvement through selective agency. What is contended for is, however, a change in our evolutionary perspective, laying increased importance upon the definiteness and cumulativeness of the internal variation, and consequently a diminished stress upon the external selection which plays on this." (*Chapters in Modern Botany*, pp. 125, 126.)

The theory that makes natural selection all-sufficient has thus bound itself to discover utilities everywhere. It assumes that every modification has been of advantage to the species.   Dr. Romanes has gone so far as to say for that species alone : " Amid all the millions of mechanisms and instincts in the animal kingdom there is no instance of a mechanism or instinct occurring in the species for the exclusive benefit of another species, although there are a few cases in which a mechanism or instinct that is of benefit to its possessor has come also to be utilised by other species. . . . How magnificent a display of Divine beneficence would organic nature have afforded if all, or even some, species had been so inter-related as to minister to each other's necessities ! " (*The Scientific Evidences of Organic Evolution*, p. 75.) " Every species," he adds, " is for itself, and for itself alone—an outcome of the always and everywhere fiercely raging struggle for life."   This was written a dozen years ago, and we do not know whether Dr. Romanes would write the same words now ; for a good deal has happened since then. Many instances have been since discovered of beings so inter-related as to minister to each other's necessities. There is the discovery of " the intimate partnership known as symbiosis, illustrated by the union of algoid and fungoid elements to form a lichen, by the occurrence of minute Algæ as constant internal associates and helpful partners of Radiolarians and some Cœlenterates." The beautiful chapter in Professor Geddes' little book *Chapters in Modern Botany* in which he describes the "web of life" contains many examples of this mutual co-operation, and of the mutual benefit resulting from it. The partnership is of benefit to both parties, and each is for the other. Professor Geddes quotes the following from De Bary : " As the result of my researches, all these growths (lichens) are not simple plants, not individuals in the ordinary sense of the word ; they are rather colonies consisting of hundreds and thousands of individuals, among which, however, one predominates, while the rest in perpetual captivity prepare the nutriment for themselves and their masters. The master is a fungus, a parasite which is accustomed to live upon others' work ; its slaves are green algæ, which it has sought out, or indeed caught hold of, and compelled into its service. It surrounds them, as a spider its prey, with a fibrous net of narrow meshes, which is gradually converted into an impenetrable covering ; but while the spider sucks its prey and leaves it dead, the fungus incites the algæ found in its net to more rapid activity, indeed to more vigorous increase." (*Chapters in Modern Botany*, p. 115.)

This is one instance of what Dr. Romanes desired, of beings so inter-related as to minister to each other's necessities. Do not the works of Darwin abound with instances of the same kind ? If insects have made flowers, and flowers have made insects, have we not another instance of the same kind ? As a matter of fact, animal life is dependent on vegetable life, and vegetable has to lift the food of animals to a higher chemical level, or animal life could not exist. This, however, may be an instance of what Dr. Romanes calls " being utilised by another species." But it could not have been utilised unless there was a fitness for use. But the same thing cannot be said of the co-operation between the bull's horn Acacia and the ants which tenant it. There is a partnership between the ants and the tree: the tree provides food and shelter for the ants, and the ants defend it from its enemies. Instead of the fiercely raging struggle for existence of which Dr. Romanes speaks, and of the mere individualism and selfishness of species which he describes as characteristic of every species, another view is gaining ground—viz., that which looks on nature as a gigantic system of mutual co-operation; each thing and species not for itself, but for others as well. The individual for the species and the species for the genus is a view which seems to be making way, as men are getting better acquainted with the intricate inter-relations of the web of life.

Co-operation demonstrably abounds ; and if it can be shown to be true, we might again find that Dr. Romanes has been brought over to the side of beneficent design as a verifiable hypothesis. " The tendency of the day is to recognise that most plants require the aid of some lower organisms for assimilating nitrogen. Thus B. Frank, who has been working for years in that direction, has proved that the beech can thrive only when a mantle of Mycorhiza-fungi develops over its roots, and that these fungi are not parasites living upon the substance of the roots, but real feeders of the beech. They obtain their food from the soil, and while so doing they yield a part of it to the roots of the tree. Further experiments of the same botanist have now shown that the same is true for the pine, which can only thrive in a soil already containing germs of the little fungi, and when its roots become covered with the mantle of fungi, while it leads but a precarious existence in the opposite case.

"All these are but separate instances of a much more general fact, which only recently became known under the general name of 'symbiosis,' and appears to have an immense significance in nature. Higher plants depend upon lower fungi and bacteria for the supply of that important part of their tissues, nitrogen. Lower fungi associate with unicellular algæ to form that great division of the vegetable world, the lichens. More than a hundred different species of algæ are already known to live in the tissues of other plants, and even in the tissues and cells of animals, and to render each other mutual services. And so on. Associations of high or low organisms are discovered every day ; and when the conditions of life are more closely examined, the whole cycle of life changes its aspect and acquires a much deeper signification." (Prince Krapotkin in *Nineteenth Century*, August 1893.) It is to be hoped, as political economy is changing its aspect in these latter days, and is learning to attach less importance to competition and more to co-operation, that those conceptions which biology has derived from political economy will also change. As products may increase in a greater degree than the people that produce them, so it may be in nature also ; and the struggle for existence may neither be so keen nor so fierce as we have supposed it to be. We see in many cases that species, instead of striving for itself, may find its advantage in mutual co-operation.

I do not intend to say much on variation. It would appear that the idea of indefinite variation is becoming antiquated, and that of definite variation coming more and more to the front. But there will apparently be some time ere the laws of definite variation can be formulated. Professor Huxley says : " The importance of natural selection will not be impaired, even if further inquiries should prove that variability is definite, and is determined in certain directions rather than in others by conditions inherent in that which varies " (*Darwiniana*, p. 223). If the inherent tendencies to variation be discovered, we shall get rid of those appeals to fortuitous variation which cause such perplexity. These laws of variation will also help us to a new conception of order and stability, and give a new meaning to design. It was in the interests of order, design, and purpose that the doctrine of special creation was prized. But a variation determined in certain directions will restore more than the denial of special creations has taken away. It leads us on to see the working out of the wonderful unity of plan in the millions of diverse living constructions, and the modifications of similar apparatus to serve diverse ends. Such a unity of plan certainly suggests the existence of thought behind the unity and manifested in it.

Professor Huxley has shown that mechanism and teleology are not mutually exclusive. He has said that a primordial molecular arrangement may have been intended to evolve the phenomena of the universe. May we not go further, and say that the existence of a plan implies not only a primordial arrangement by which the plan can be realised, but also that the Power to which the plan is due is never absent from the working out of it ? A power present in the world, who works according to a plan, and by which the plan can become real, gives us something which we can understand, which also delivers us from the tyranny of chance. The process of realising the plan embodied in nature has been slow, and step by step; but, then, the end has so far been accomplished. And it is a curious result to which many have come, that when we have discovered so far the means by which the plan has been wrought out, we have therefore denied, not that there is a plan, but that there is a mind, a reason which made the plan and carried it out. It is as if we denied the existence of the architect after we had seen the stones and the timber, the mason, the hodman, and the joiner at work. Or is it that we deny the planning intelligence because the building has not sprung suddenly into existence? The wise Bishop has depicted that state of mind in his own inimitable way : " Men are impatient, and for precipitating things; but the Author of nature appears deliberate throughout His operations, accomplishing His natural ends by slow successive steps " (*Analogy*, Part II., chap. iv.).

Our friends and teachers have shown us innumerable adaptations; they have shown us that the creatures work towards an end—an end not foreseen by the individuals or the species concerned ; we therefore hold that it must have been foreseen by some one, if causation is to have its due place. We are constrained, on the other hypothesis, to ask how unintelligent laws can work out intelligible and intelligent results. We can never get an answer to that question; for the postulation of a Supreme Intelligence cannot be tested by experiment, because it is assumed by all experiments. Every experiment assumes that we are in a rational universe, a universe the working of which corresponds to the working of an intelligence in ourselves. If the laws of nature work out intelligent and rational results, then reason is at work in them. We have not put the intelligibility into the world; we find it there, and we strive to understand and to express the working of the world in rational terms,—an attempt which would be for ever vain, if the intelligence at work in the world were not of the same kind as the intelligence which is at work in ourselves.

It may be true that the intelligence at work in the world has not wrought in the fashion we had supposed. Does that intelligence work by the way of evolution, and not in the particular mode we thought of?—for a change of conception may not be the destruction of the conception. The earth is a part of the solar system—men once thought it the centre of things; we no longer think of personal spirits as guides and rulers of the stars—we think of matter under gravitation; we have been taught that species did not arise through special acts of creation, but were developed one after the other. Well, we bow our heads in reverence, and say that God's ways are not as our ways, and His thoughts are not as our thoughts; but they are ways and thoughts of God notwithstanding. If we trace the highest results of the world to the humblest and most simple beginnings, we do not destroy the value and interest of anything when we know how it came about. The more we learn of the methods of the world's development, the more is our feeling of wonder enhanced, and the larger does our conception grow of the Divine method; for at every stage of the process we find powers at work which were not at work in the lower stage. From the mechanical we arrive at the chemical, from the chemical to the organic, and from the organic we reach the conscious stage of existence. We confessedly cannot explain the chemical by the physical, nor the organic by the chemical and the mechanical, nor the conscious by what is unconscious. If, then, we have arrived at the goal of conscious, moral, social, religious life, we have come to a stage in which a philosophy, a science, a moral system, a creed ought to be possible.

CHAPTER VIII

SUPER-ORGANIC EVOLUTION

Controversy regarding heredity—Spencer and Weismann—
Machinery of Evolution defective—Limits of Organic
Evolution—Man does not modify himself, but modifies
his Environment—Survival of the Fittest explained by
Huxley and by Spencer—Evolution does not account for
advance—Illustration of man's power of modifying his
environment—Results.

IT is with some timidity that one ventures at the
present time to write the word " heredity." It
is one of the three great names which occur in
connection with evolution. " Variability," " natural
selection," transmission or " heredity," are words which
occur in every statement of the theory of evolution,
and both the meaning and causes of each are keenly
contested. At present the contest is keenly waged
as to the nature and the meaning and the factors of
heredity. The problem is, no doubt, a most complex
one, and there are great biological authorities who
widely differ as to what is transmitted and the
means of transmission. Are acquired qualities—that
is, qualities acquired in the lifetime of an individual
—transmitted to his offspring? Weismann and
Lankester deny the transmissibility of acquired
qualities, and contend that only inborn, germinal,

or constitutional variations are transmissible; while Mr. Herbert Spencer emphatically says that "either there has been inheritance of acquired characters, or there has been no evolution" (*Contemporary Review*, March 1893, p. 446). And again he says: "A right answer to the question whether acquired characters are or are not inherited underlies right beliefs, not only in biology and psychology, but also in education, ethics, and politics" (May 1893, p. 730). The question, like many other questions, was raised by Darwin, whose theory of pangenesis had the supreme merit, not of solving the problem, but of showing how great, complex, and intricate was the problem that needed to be solved.

Not many have believed in pangenesis, but pangenesis has set men to inquire into the nature and character of inheritance. What is the relation between successive generations? What is the character of the organic continuity which all alike recognise as a fact? Have the experience, character, and aquirements of individuals any chance of being transmitted to their offspring? It seems best to me to wait for an answer. If a man of the scientific attainments of Dr. Romanes can say, "Professor Weismann is not quite correct in saying that I adhere to the doctrine of the transmission of acquired characters. My position with regard to this question is one of suspended judgment," one less expert may well be excused for remaining in suspense. We may watch the evolution of the controversy with interest. We may read the writings of Professor Weismann as these are printed from year to year; and whether his main contention is made out or not, we always gain some knowledge from him. We may listen with sympathy to the complaints of Mr. J. T. Cunningham when he states that he has been boycotted by *Nature*. " *Nature*," he says, " has embraced the principles of Weismann's Neo-Darwinism ; and while willing to devote plenty of space to favourable reviews of Weismann's essays written by undergraduates, suppresses without a word of explanation or apology contributions which argue against the fashionable creed" (Translator's preface to Eimer's *Organic Evolution*, p. xxii.). And we ask ourselves, Has the *odium theologicum* been suddenly transferred to science ? Or we may read the mild and reasonable and able summary of the whole question in Mr. Arthur Thomson's book *The Study of Animal Life*, which is so clear and lucid that a non-specialist may readily understand the issue. We may read the controversy between Herbert Spencer and Professor Weismann, their statements and replies and rejoinders in the *Contemporary Review* of 1893, and mark the keenness of the conflict and the fierceness of the attack and defence, and be thankful that we can stand aside and take no part in it. We may wait until the controversy is settled, and apparently the issue may be decided in the next century. Happily for our purpose it is not necessary to wait for the cessation of the controversy. It is enough for us that there is a relation of organic unity between the generations, and it is not necessary for us to decide for our purpose as to the precise machinery by which the organic continuity is maintained. Mr. Spencer is bound to fight hard for the transmission of acquired characters; for it is on that supposition that he has formulated his system of psychology and ethics, and has propounded his scheme of reconciliation between *a priori* and *a posteriori* forms of knowledge. We need not here controvert his theory of inheritance; for on our view, even if granted, it does not prove his case. No doubt Weismann also, if he ever reaches the study of psychology and ethics, would have his explanation from his own point of view.

Meanwhile, while the machinery of evolution is so far defective, and men are not agreed as to what heredity is, we may at least assume as true that the results won by organic modification have somehow been preserved. Things have really made progress. Species have been produced, and once produced they beget others in their own likeness. Life may have gone on irrespective of the experience of the individual, as Weismann says; or the experience and acquirements of the individual have played a respectable part in evolutionary progress, as Mr. Spencer says; still, life has gone on, and has got itself sorted into certain kinds.

Organic modification is, however, an expensive process, and cannot go on for ever; for life to continue to inscribe its experience in cells, be these cells and their functions as varied and diversified as we please, is a process which has a limit. We know not, and scarcely any one can guess, what power and potency may be in a living cell. It may carry within it the potency of a Shakespeare or of a Newton. But our aim at present is to show that the process of organic change has become less and less as life has become more and more complicated. Organically the difference between unicellular and multicellular beings seems to be greater than any subsequent organic change. Nor have biologists yet been able to account for the transmission from simple to complex organisms. Indeed, it is sometimes hard to justify the kind of language with which biologists describe certain beings. According to the Darwinian theory it is the fittest which always survive. The unfit can never survive on that view. But we constantly read of " degeneration," and sometimes the hermit-crab receives a good deal of abuse because it has ceased to produce its own shell. Then parasites receive a good deal of abuse. On the Darwinian theory all this is quite unjustifiable. The survival of degraded forms, as they are called, and the shift for a living which leads to parasitism are also instances of the survival of the fittest.

On the one hand, the principle of Darwinism would seem to shut us out from the use of words like degeneration ; and on the other hand, it should also cause us to avoid the use of " progress," and words of a similar meaning. Our judgment on organisms must be expressed in terms of the theory ; but on these terms a good deal of Darwinian literature would require to be re-written. For the idea of progress we need some other criterion than is given us by the "survival of the fittest " ; for many lower organisms survive. The scorpion has been in evidence ever since the coal measures have been laid down ; and others also survive. Have we any explanation in the principle of the survival of the fittest of the appearance of the higher races, as we call them ? for the survival proves the fitness, and it proves nothing more. Professor Huxley is plain on this matter, and Mr. Herbert Spencer is also equally plain. Professor Huxley says: "'Fittest' has a connotation of 'best'; and about 'best' there hangs a moral flavour. In cosmic nature, however, what is fittest depends upon the conditions. Long since I ventured to point out that if our hemisphere were to cool again, the survival of the fittest might bring about, in the vegetable kingdom, a population of more and more stunted and humbler and humbler organisms, until the fittest that survived might be nothing but lichens, diatoms, and such microscopic organisms as those which give red snow its colour ; while, if it became hotter, the pleasant valleys of the Thames and Isis might be uninhabitable by any animated beings save those that flourish in a tropical jungle. They, as the fittest, the best adapted to the changed conditions, might survive." (*The Romanes Lecture*, 1893, p. 32.)

Mr. Spencer says: "Mr. Martineau speaks of the 'survivorship of the better,' as though that were the statement of the law, and then adds that the alleged result cannot be inferred 'except on the assumption that whatever is *better* is *stronger* too.' But the words he here uses are his own words, not the words of those he opposes. The law is the survival of the *fittest*. Probably, in substituting 'better' for fittest, Mr. Martineau did not suppose that he was changing the meaning; though I dare say he perceived that the meaning of the word fittest did not suit his argument so well. Had he examined the facts he would have found that the law is not the survival of the 'better' or the 'stronger,' if we give to those words anything like their ordinary meanings. It is the survival of those which are constitutionally fittest to thrive under the conditions in which they are placed; and very often that which, humanly speaking, is inferiority, causes the survival. Superiority, whether in size, strength, activity, or sagacity, is, other things equal, at the cost of diminished fertility; and when the life led by a species does not demand these higher attributes, the species profits by decrease of them and accompanying increase of fertility. This is the reason why there occur so many cases of retrograde metamorphosis —this is the reason why parasites, internal or external, are so commonly degraded forms of higher types. Survival of the 'better' does not cover these cases, though survival of the 'fittest' does." (*Essays*, vol. iii., pp. 241, 242.) Many things might be said on these two extracts. One thing to be noticed is the use of language not derived from evolution. What is the ground of judgment which warrants Professor Huxley in speaking of "humbler and humbler organisms," and Mr. Spencer in speaking of a "retrograde metamorphosis" and of "inferiority"? In the "survival of the fittest" we have the only criterion by which we can judge, and to use other terms is to bring back surreptitiously principles which we have discarded.

There is something else to be said which is more relevant. On the theory as stated by Professor Huxley and Mr. Spencer, there is no provision for progress, nor any machinery provided which even can seem to lead to that advance which life has made from the protozoa up to man. The protozoa have survived because they are the fittest. Why, then, has life advanced to other forms? Surely a principle the working of which is consistent with the survival of all that have survived cannot explain why some forms have survived unchanged and others have changed! The same principle is inadequate for the explanation of both. What, then, is the principle which has secured advance? Variability in all directions cannot account for it, for the likelihood is that changes will cancel one another. Heredity will not account for it, since changes must be of a kind to survive before they can be perpetuated and accumulated. Shall we not be driven back, by the very principle of the survival of the fittest, to postulate some other principle which will ensure advance? Can we get that principle within the organism itself, in laws of growth, in the nature of life itself, in the interactions of life with the environment, or any other of the means postulated by the biologist? At all events, the principle has not yet been discovered, and we may wait for its discovery with some patience. It does not appear that for a rational understanding of the progress which life has made we can yet dispense with the hypothesis of Energising Reason that foresees the end and goal, knows what it would be at, and takes adequate means to secure its end. Energising Reason is also one of the causes which can be seen at work in the universe at present, and we may ask our scientific friends to recognise its reality. It is one of the causes now at work in the universe; and may we not say that it has always been at work, since we find ourselves in a rational universe?

On any view, however, man is the crown and goal of the organic world, and in him the organic world has come to know itself. At present we shall not seek to look at the question of his descent, or rather of his ascent, from the organic world to self-consciousness. We shall look at him first in his relation to and his contrast with the world beneath him; for since man has been on the earth he has been distinctively man. "When we study this fossil man of the quaternary period, who must, of course, have stood comparatively near to our primitive ancestors in the order of descent or ascent, we always find a *Man*, just such as men are now" (Virchow, *The Freedom of Science*, p. 60). As far back as we can trace him man is man, and wherever we find him we find that the method of advance by mere organic modification has been distinctly limited; for the organic differences between varieties of the human family are insignificant in comparison with the number of elements in which they are one. The differences are only superficial and external, and a savage may in the course of a single lifetime become a civilised man. Physically, therefore, and also in many other respects, man is one.

Physically, notwithstanding the great general likeness between man and the higher animals, there is a distinct difference; for man has the power of modifying his environment, and only in a slight degree does he need to modify himself. He does not need to develop defensive armour against the attacks of wild beasts, does not require to don scales against his enemy as the crocodile does, nor grow sharp teeth and claws as the tiger does, nor to mimic offensive and nauseous qualities as the butterflies seem to do. He does not need to be so strong, or so swift, or so cunning as other animals. He has found ways less expensive than organic modification, and he has acted on them. He does not need to lengthen or to strengthen his arm in order to be able to lift heavy weights; he has in effect done both by discovering and utilising the lever. His eye is not so keen as the eye of the eagle; but with an eye less keen he can see farther, for he has discovered the telescope. His eye may not be so fitted for microscopic vision as that of a fly ; but he can see things so small as to be invisible to the eye of any other creature. He cannot spring so far as a tiger can ; but he has discovered that a rifle bullet is swifter than a tiger's leap and stronger than a tiger's muscles. In short, he has ceased to modify his physical organism, having found out that he can succeed as well by modifying tools and weapons and making them serve his purpose.

In winter many animals have to modify themselves to protect themselves from cold. They put on a thicker fleece of fur, and many of them change their colour. Who can say what is the physiological cost of the heavier fur ? or the amount of energy expended in the organic change ? But man simply puts on a thicker overcoat, which he can easily slip off when warmer weather comes—a process which involves no physiological cost. Not many animals can modify their environment. They build their nests, they seek out dens and caves of the earth, or they may use other means of a simpler sort to protect themselves.

But man has learnt to build houses, to warm them with fire, to supply himself with light when the sun goes down, and in a hundred other ways to make a climate at his pleasure. He can cook his food, and save a large part of the physiological labour of digestion. He can also provide for the future—sow seed in the spring, gather it in harvest, and store it up for future use. In this he has no doubt been anticipated by the ants, but almost all other animals live from day to day.

Not only has he ceased to modify himself, and modifies his environment instead; he has pressed the organic modifications of other animals into his service. He has directed the modifications of certain grasses until he has produced wheat. He has taken animals and moulded them into a form which makes them of greater use to him. He makes use of the swiftness of the horse, and of the qualities of other animals which he has tamed and made submissive to his wishes. He has chained the lightning, he has harnessed steam to his carriage, and there is hardly any limit to the use he has made and is still making of the agents and powers of the world.

These things he has done because he has been able to rise above the necessity of organic modification Other creatures are under the necessity of modifying themselves to meet the changing conditions of life; and if the modification succeeds, they transmit it to the species. The whole process is organic, and unless the modification becomes so organic as to be transmitted it is lost. Memory with them seems also to be organic. The experience of the individual does not seem to count for much ; what counts is that habit that has got itself inwrought into their nature and has become instinctive. While there are still habit and instinct in man, they do not play so great a part as in the lower stages of life. At all events, the powers which animals have of recording their experience, profiting by it, and transmitting it are very limited. As with tools and weapons and houses and garments, so also with the power of recording and transmitting experience, man has found a more excellent and a more economic way. He does not inscribe his experience in the convolutions of the brain ; he writes them in a book, and books are less expensive than brains, and the supply of book-material is much more ample and more easily procurable than brain-matter. It is also more lasting; for brains vanish with the individual, and books last for all time. Hereditary transmission is precarious, and may not, indeed cannot, hand down the largest and greatest of human possessions. The greatest and most valuable of human experiences may have belonged to a man who had no offspring, and thus would inevitably have been lost had man not found out a way of recording it. Organic memory would not lead to much, and along with other organic modifications tends to decrease in man. But this new way of recording experience has obvious advantages. Homer's song has lasted ; but it would have perished had organic memory been the only link between the generations. The thoughts of Plato and of Aristotle, the song of Dante, the *Principia* of Newton are with us still, because man has speech, and intelligence, and ways of recording and transmitting that experience, apart from a series of organic changes in the individual and in the species. It is not needful to write more at length on this point; for we have our art, our science, our literature, our architecture, our philosophy, our poetry, our theology, each one of which, and much more all of them together, tell us and prove to us that here in man there is a new kind of life—a life that has not changed with the changing environment, but has so far altered the environment to suit its own ends.

We have simply looked at man as a being who has his place among other beings on this earth. We have not denied his similarity to other animals. We have not looked for structural, or physiological, or other differences between him and other animated beings. We have raised no question as to his origin, or his relation to the world of life which preceded him. We have simply looked at him and at them, in themselves, in their actions, and in their results; and we have found ourselves burdened with a load of distinctions and differences, and we ask for an explanation of them. We have found much instruction in the works of Darwin on the *Descent of Man* and on the *Expression of the Emotions.* And we have read Dr. Romanes with profit as he toils and struggles at an impossible task, namely, to trace the evolution of intelligence through animals up to man without a break. Dr. Tylor's work also is full of interest as he strives to trace for us the origin and growth of language, and the rise and progress of the arts of life. But there is a marked difference between this kind of evolution and that kind with which we are familiar in the organic world. Here it is not the physical organism that is evolved; it is something else. No one will say that there is a growth of the human brain or the nervous system which proceeds *pari passu* with the evolution of tools, of languages, of civilisation. Virchow's statement already quoted is destructive of that supposition. If in all physical characteristics man is man from the time when he first appears on the earth, then the evolution of arts, science, civilisation has not been accompanied by corresponding organic changes. It would be well to recognise this, and for mental progress to devise a formula of evolution not now expressed in terms of matter and motion, but in terms of mind and reason. Not that we can dispense with mind and reason in the case of physical and organic development, for in it are discovered all the principles of a rational order; but in the latter kind of evolution both the order and the method of it and the thing which is developed can be expressed in terms of mind alone.

The essential note of difference appears at the point where a being appears who can adapt himself to the environment, not by changing himself, but by changing the environment. The beginning of the change may be very small; but the main point to observe is that a change has been begun. The lower animals indeed have "rudiments of the implement-using faculty. Orangs in the Durian trees furiously pelt passers-by with the thorny fruit. The chimpanzee in the forests is said to crack nuts with a stone." And the first tools which man uses are likely those which are ready-made or which can be finished for use. But no animal, as far as we know, ever gives just the finish, slight or great, which the tool requires to fit it for use. When man first carried a pebble about with him as a weapon of offence, when he used a sharp stone to cut or scrape with, or shaped the branch of a tree for use as a club, he made a new departure. We may, if we like, trace the growing use of tools and weapons, as Dr. Tylor does in his *Anthropology*, and see how man learned to use better and better material for his tools and weapons, and to make better and better implements. We may trace the improvements in the line of offence and defence, until we pass from the stone weapon to an Armstrong gun; or we may trace the development of industrial implements from the first rude implement with which man scratched the earth, until we come to the steam plough and the reaping machine; or trace the evolution of dwellings from the cave and the shelter under a tree to the homes of the present day, with their comfort, refinement, beauty; and we may also trace other lines of development: but we ought always to remember that this is a peculiar line of development. It is the first step that counts, and the first step was taken with the first tool which man fashioned, with the first garment he wore, with the first shelter he made for himself. For the lower animals, as for man, the wealth of the world existed, if they could use it. And they did use it after their fashion; but they had to use their environment as it was, and adapt themselves to it. Their weapons of offence and defence were organic, and they could adapt themselves to the conditions of life only with exceeding slowness. This holds true even if we accept all that is told us of the exceeding cunning of animals, and of the manifoldness of the shifts they have to make for a living. Accept all that Mr. Poulton tells us about the colours of animals, and his explanation of mimicry and its advantages, and the remark yet holds good that mimicry has succeeded just because it was so far organic. The mimickers had to make the changes which procured them an advantage by some modification of shape, of colour, or of attitude, or in some way they were physically modified. It may be true also that the change was slight and did not become structural; but the change was effected by a modification of its own substance, and not by the use of something else.

There are many instances, indeed, which look like an anticipation of the unique power of man to modify his environment. Mr. Poulton quotes from Mr. Bateson as follows: "The crab takes a piece of weed in his two chelæ, and, neither scratching nor biting it, deliberately tears it across, as a man tears paper with his hands. He then puts one end of it into his mouth, and after chewing it up, presumably to soften it, takes it out in the chelæ and rubs it firmly on his head or legs until it is caught by the peculiar curved hairs which cover them. If the piece of weed is not caught by the hairs, the crab puts it back in its mouth and chews it up again. The whole proceeding is most human and purposeful." (*Colour of Animals*, pp. 78, 79.) There are other instances also of what Mr. Arthur Thomson calls "masking," in which use is made of external things for purposes of concealment and protection ; and there may be other instances in which animals may, without organic modification, succeed in concealing and protecting themselves. However these may be explained, it is broadly true that one distinction between human life and other life is this power of which we have spoken—the power of making other things serve the purpose of life. And this power has grown from more to more, until we can really set no limit to the process of change due to the action of man. There may come a time when man may prepare his food directly from inorganic elements, and may dispense with the agency of plants and animals needed at present, in order that his food may be raised to the chemical level at which he is able to use it. Speaking broadly, therefore, the power of modifying his environment, and particularly the power of doing it progressively and with ever-increasing success, belongs to man alone of all the forms of life on the earth.

As there are limits set to the power of organic modification, so also are there limits to the nature of heredity in relation to man. Of the accumulated intellectual, emotional, moral, and spiritual treasures of humanity, not much is due to the cumulative power of hereditary action. Parents do not transmit to their children the knowledge which they have themselves obtained. Children have by slow and painful methods to learn even to walk and to run, and much more have they to learn grammar, arithmetic, mathematics, the arts and sciences, ethics, and philosophy. Nor can it be said that even special aptitudes are transmitted; for a mathematician may have sons who are far from being mathematical. It would seem that, in the advance of humanity, education counts for more than heredity. Besides on the new line of advance which man has discovered, we find a new distinction between man and the lower animals. Their hereditary transmissions are limited to what has become organic, and to what has come to them by the particular line of their own ancestry. An ape has no way of receiving the transmitted organised experience of all apes; he obtains only what has been handed down by his own direct predecessors. There may be varieties of attainment among the family of apes. One may be wiser, stronger, more courageous than others; but, supposing that these can be transmitted, they can be transmitted only to his immediate and direct progeny. But with man, and with the new means of transmission he has discovered, nothing need be lost. What has been won by one man may become the inheritance of the race; for the race of man is one in a sense which can belong to no other species. And the achievement of one race may become the common property of all the races of man. Whatever finer feelings or deeper cunning may have belonged to an exceptional animal perishes with him; but the services rendered to humanity by " the dead but sceptred sovrans who still rule our spirits from their urns" are recorded and are living and powerful to-day. Individual men differ from one another in many respects, but all humanity is in every man. Some may fall below the average, but others rise high above it, and may reveal to us how great humanity is. The great men of humanity have given to it possessions which man will not wittingly let die. They have lifted us up to the heights of knowledge, of feeling, of volition. The truth and beauty they have seen they have also recorded, and succeeding men may live on what they have handed down.

Organic modification seems to have no way of preserving these exceptional experiences, and therefore the lower animals must be still subject to that complex of conditions which serves to produce organic changes. But these laws of variability, natural selection, and heredity have, in man, given place to other and higher laws of development. How the thought of one man may help to enable other men to be adapted to environment let the history of civilisation testify. One man thinks the steam engine, and suddenly the conditions of modern life are changed for all men. One might speak here of the poets and their gift of song to the race, of the painters who have revealed to their fellow-men the Divine quality of beauty in the world, of the scientific leaders of the generations who have wrested from nature the laws of her movements both in the heavens above and in the earth beneath, of the thinkers of philosophy who have aspired to think in human thought and express in human language the thought which is embodied in the universe and in all its movements. Take the great men of the world, who have been the mightiest benefactors of their race, and we may say of them and their influence that their exceptional might and power and insight would have perished with them-

selves had the evolution of man been limited to the
natural selection, heredity, and adaptation which
seem to rule in the organic world. Happily, however,
in the evolution of mental life higher laws have been
found and wider results have been won than were
possible on the old lines of development. For the
exceptional men of the world of humanity have
served the race, but their service has been of the
spiritual sort, and the transmission of their thought
and emotion was by means which were not of an
organic and mechanical kind. Nor can it be said
of them that the struggle for existence had much
part in the production of their capacity, or in the
expression of their thought. These singers sang
because they could not do otherwise. These men of
science worked and toiled because they were urged on
by some mental desire to know the secret of the
action of nature in the particular sphere of their
observation, and so of the others. For they were
urged on by their love of beauty, their passion
for truth, their desire it may be to better their
fellow-men. It may be safely said that not one or
hardly any of those great men whose thoughts and
works have helped to develop the higher side of our
nature, the intelligence, the social and moral sentiments, have ever been pressed on to this kind of work
by the struggle for existence. They spoke and toiled
because a finer necessity was laid on them. Having
seen the vision they must speak it; and they spoke,
and lifted men towards the heights on which they
dwelt. They revealed to others the depth and height
and possibility of human nature, and encouraged

ordinary human people to seek the heights where such visions could be seen.

It is evident, therefore, that the study of man must be directed differently and must recognise larger principles than we find at work in other spheres of knowledge. We do not at present raise the question of the origin of man, or ask how we are to explain the difference between him and the lower creation. All we now do is to insist on the difference, and to have some idea of what it is. The difference is there, in whatever way we account for it. We may trace the supposed path of progress from the lower organic world to man, and add one infinitesimal difference to another, and then suppose we have explained the matter. Suppose we have traced the slow steps of development, as we have not, yet the process does not explain the outcome of the process. What has to be explained, or simply accepted, is the change of method when we pass from the lower world to man. Physically the change is seen in the limitation of these laws of organic life by laws which have a larger meaning and a wider sweep. The laws of life seem to press the laws of physics and chemistry into their service, and control them for higher issues; so also the laws of mental life seem to grasp all the complexes of laws of physics, chemistry, organic life, and give them a new transformation, and direct them to ends unexpected and unforeseen, until the higher form of mental life appeared. The laws of the lower sphere are not abrogated, and do not cease to operate, nor are the properties and qualities of the lower spheres changed; but they obtain a new significance, and the unity of the universe gets a wider meaning, when all its forces are seen to be serviceable, or at least in the service of the mental life, which can see them, think them anew, understand them, and transform them with a more glorious significance. Thus we do not endeavour to explain the higher by the lower, or the effect by the cause. On the contrary, the lower can never be rightly seen until it is set in the light of what is higher ; and the cause is never seen in its breadth, and length, and depth, and height until we see what it can do, and that we see only in the effect.

CHAPTER IX

EVOLUTION AND PSYCHOLOGY

Human and animal intelligence—Rational Self-consciousness —Habit—Feelings, Emotions, Appetites in rational beings and irrational—Differences in Kind and in Degree— Romanes and Spencer—Can feelings make a consciousness?—The Self-Genesis of self according to Romanes and Spencer—Unity of human nature—Russel Wallace's Deistic view—Creation is continuous—Results.

WHAT we have seen with regard to the action of man in modifying his environment appears even more plainly when we consider his mental life. From the consideration of his mental life we shall gather that he is a unique being, with notes and characteristics which are only foreshadowed in the lower world of animals. That there are such foreshadowings it would be idle to deny. There are in the lower creation adaptations which seem to be unconscious, such as the colours of animals, and many others which cannot be ascribed to the purpose and will of the animals concerned. But there are other actions and adaptations of which the only explanation is that they were purposely intended by the animals who did them. Whoever reads such works as those of Dr. Romanes on *Animal Intelligence* will at once admit that the question is beyond dispute. Animals are intelligent; but their intelligence is of a rudimentary kind. The only question which is of interest here is, Can we explain human intelligence as if it were the same in kind as the intelligence we see in the ant and the elephant, and in other animals? Can we substitute for the higher nature the laws and processes of the narrower non-human world, and explain the higher by the lower? We may say that the higher is evolved from the lower. Suppose we do. It is just the evolution that has to be explained; for when we come to human nature we come to a nature which is consciously rational. And when conscious reason has appeared, there is a difference between the attitudes and relations of the conscious being and those which seem to be like them in the being which is not rational. While the stimulus which gives rise to sensation and the sensation itself may be alike in the animal and the man, yet the reaction against the stimulus is very different. The fact that man is a rational and self-conscious being makes every feeling, every emotion, every volition of a different order. In the lower organisms the reaction on stimulus is simple and uniform, and the appropriate action follows almost immediately. As organisms advance in complexity, and as the nervous system becomes more elaborate, the reaction gets to be more slow and full of purpose, until we come to the actions of the ant, or of the other more intelligent animals; for every single being is a unity, and capable of reaction to stimulus.

When we come to speak of a rational self-conscious being, the reaction partakes of the whole nature of the being; and an element of rationality enters into every response which the rational being makes to its environment. The stimulus is referred to the self-conscious being, and the response is that of the self-conscious being. This is true even when the response has become automatic; for automatic action seems for man to be a secondary product. Actions learned with effort by continued and repeated and conscious action of attention grow easier by repetition, and are at length performed without any attention at all. A large part of man's habitual action is thus handed over, as it were, to mechanism, and stimulus and reaction become so co-ordinated that we can do our work without constant superintendence. We are thus set free for further attainment. Reason and attention have made the habit, and can now proceed to something else.

It would take too much space to lead a detailed proof of the statement that the feelings, the emotions, even the appetites of a rational being, have taken into themselves new elements which differentiate them from the experiences of the animals which have not risen to a consciousness of self. Take the appetites themselves, and a little reflection will show that even here a new element has entered in. Man can control his appetites, can accustom himself to new kinds of food, can make an element of reason enter into the preparation of his food. He can make it, or at least can so modify it as to make it serve his purpose better. The stimulus of hunger and of thirst physiologically considered may be one in man, and in an animal the response to it is different by all the breadth which separates the rational nature from that which is

not rational. And if appetite becomes a new thing
with rational beings, much more is this true of the
emotions. Take the table prefixed by Dr. Romanes
to his works on *Mental Evolution in Animals* and
Mental Evolution in Man, and let us assume that these
emotions are manifested by animals. He claims that
animals can manifest surprise, fear, parental affection,
jealousy, affection, sympathy, emulation, grief, revenge,
shame, and remorse; and he affirms that they resemble,
or that they are the same in kind, as those emotions
which are called by the same name in man. His
proof consists in an interpretation of the sign of
an emotion which appears when the animals are in
the state which seems to correspond to it. Thus he
interprets the sign of anger as he would interpret it
in man. Well, we are not to urge the difficulty of
interpreting these signs, inasmuch as we are not mere
animals, and cannot enter into the consciousness of
animals. Dr. Romanes knows this preliminary difficulty, and has taken care to keep his interpretation
within the mark. Let us suppose that the signs of
fear, surprise, and all the other emotions are the
same in animals and in man, and also that the
feelings as mere feelings are identical; yet in the case
of man the feelings are taken up into the web of
conscious rational experience, and are shot through
with that quality that reason gives, while the experience of the other remains irrational. Let us remember
that feelings are a relation between the stimuli and
the being which has the feeling. A feeling is not
something in itself, unrelated, unrecognised; it is the
response of the living being to the stimulus. And the

relation between different feelings is just the relation which each has to the subject of them.

The emotion of surprise, to take the one lowest on Dr. Romanes' list, is one thing with the lower animals and another thing with man. What it is will depend on the experience and wisdom of the being who experiences it. In fact, the emotion of surprise differs in man according to the culture, knowledge, and experience of the man. We are not surprised at the existence of railways, telegraphs, telephones; our fathers would have felt the utmost surprise if they had seen them. The ancients felt no surprise at the notion of a hippocentaur; we should feel the utmost surprise if we saw one. It is evident, therefore, that the emotion of surprise has with man now a deeper character, a more rational element than it had in former ages. Where it does exist it has a wider meaning, and has gathered into itself the wider knowledge, the deeper experience of the rational man. If emotions in the human family can thus be built up of more complex elements as the ages pass on, shall we not also say that the emotions of man are also more complex than those of the irrational creatures? We cannot isolate the emotions, and think of them as if they took place in a vacuum. The simplest feelings partake of the complexity of the whole being.

It appears to me, therefore, that much of the writing of Darwin in *The Descent of Man* and in *The Expression of the Emotions* is irrelevant to the purpose he has in hand. He first would have to show that the emotions in the lower animals are identical with those in man. He has assumed without inquiring that, when he has got the same muscular contraction, say, of the forehead in the monkey and in man, he has also got the same subjective state. But this is incapable of proof ; it seems, indeed, to be capable of disproof. The outward signs may seem to be identical, but the inward feeling may be as wide as the poles asunder. That which is what it is in relation to a whole is to be judged in relation to the whole of which it is a part. And an emotion is to be judged in relation to the being in whose experience it is a factor ; and thus the emotion partakes of the character of that being, and will increase in complexity in proportion as the experience consists of more or less elements in relation to the whole. Thus the emotion of a being who has not attained, and who never will attain, to self-consciousness can scarcely, to any profit, be compared with the emotions of a being who is potentially at least self-conscious from the beginning.

If it is so with the emotions, *a fortiori* it is so with the cognitions and the volitions of man. Comparative psychology can make little progress for this very reason, because the being who makes the comparison is rational, and is apt to read his own rationality into what he observes. It appears to us that Dr. Romanes has not been able to avoid this cause of uncertainty. In his able and interesting books already mentioned he has done more than any other man in the attempt to prove that the intelligence of animals is the same in kind as the intelligence in man, though he admits a difference in degree. It is not easy to make out what Dr. Romanes means by a difference in kind, or rather it is difficult to say whether Dr. Romanes

would admit that any difference is a difference in kind.
We have the following note from him : " It is perhaps
desirable to explain from the first that by the words
' difference of kind,' as used in the above paragraph
and elsewhere throughout this treatise, I mean difference of *origin*. This is the only real distinction that
can be drawn between the terms ' difference of kind '
and ' difference of degree,' and I should have scarcely
have deemed it worth while to give the definition, had
it not been for the confused manner in which the
terms are used by some writers—*e.g.*, Professor Sayce,
who says, while speaking of languages from a common
source, ' differences of degree become in time differences
of kind.' " (*Mental Evolution in Man*, p. 3 note.)

Can there be on Dr. Romanes' terms a difference of
kind ? On his own view, the view of evolution, any
distinction between species and species can never be a
distinction of kind, for it can never be a " difference
of origin." All the forms of animals have been modified to their present shape by slow changes—that is,
according to the teaching of Dr. Romanes. They
have one origin. Are we to say, then, that there
is no difference of kind between the vertebrate and
the invertebrate, between a salmon and an elephant,
between an ape and a man ? Are we to set down the
difference between species and species as a difference
in degree ? If not, then Professor Sayce is right in
saying that a difference in degree may become a difference in kind. It is also difficult to understand what
Dr. Romanes means by a difference of origin. We
thought that evolution had given up the search after
origins, and had discovered that it must begin with

something. According to the theory of Mr. Spencer, we begin with an Unknowable Power, and the first form of its manifestation lay in the primitive nebulosity. If we take the more modest form of the Darwinian hypothesis, we still begin with life, and all life has only one origin according to him. If with Haeckel we seek to unite the living with the non-living and to bridge the chasm between the two, we still begin somewhere, and according to the theory of evolution there is one origin for everything.

It is also the view of theology. Theologians also have only one, know of only one origin for the universe, and for all that is in it. They say in the beginning God created the heavens and the earth. They believe, in the words of a book which they revere and honour and seek to obey, that " by the word of the Lord were the heavens made, and all the host of them by the breath of His mouth." They do not distinguish between man and the lower animals by a difference of origin; for all derived existence must, they believe, trace its origin to God. If the Scripture says, " God created man in His own image, in the image of God created He him; male and female created He them "; if it says, furthermore, " The Lord God formed man of the dust of the ground, and breathed into his nostrils the breath of life; and man became a living soul," it also says, " Thou sendest forth Thy Spirit, they are created, and Thou renewest the face of the ground." Thus, as far as the question of origin is concerned, there is for the theologian no question of difference of kind, all things owe their origin to the creative power of God, and all things are sustained by Him.

11

Nor for the evolutionist can there be, on Dr. Romanes'
teaching, any difference of kind; for all things are
from the primal source of being whatever that may
be, and all things are what they are by the same kind
of process. If difference of kind means difference of
origin, then there can be no difference of kind; and
we must get for ourselves some new kind of classification just to satisfy the caprice of Dr. Romanes.

What may amount to a difference in kind falls
therefore to be determined by a consideration, not of
the origin and history of a being, but by a consideration of its present nature, character, and action. If
we can say that there is a specific difference between
one class of animals and another, we have in other
words established a difference of kind. Biologists do
not, as far as I can gather, refuse to recognise a
difference of kind between one species and another ;
they do not deny a difference of species ; the main question for them has been, How came there to be a species ?
The problem of organic evolution is, given life, to show
how it has come to be sorted into different kinds. Will
Dr. Romanes help us to language which will enable us
to distinguish between one species and another ? We
shall not quarrel with him about phrases. If he
will give us a word which will express the difference
between species and species, we shall take it ; but till
then we shall say with Professor Sayce and most other
people that a difference in degree may become so
great as ultimately to amount to a difference in kind.

It is somewhat perilous to disagree with Dr. Romanes,
for every now and then we come across phrases like
the following : " This is admitted by all my opponents

who understand the psychology of the subject." Of
course the assumption is, that if we do not admit his
view we are of those who do not understand the
psychology of the subject. Recognising the peril,
we still venture to doubt and to demur to many of
his psychological assumptions. We admit that Dr.
Romanes is in the succession of English psychologists.
He follows in the wake of Locke, Priestley, Hume,
the Mills, Bain, and he seems to think that it is
the only possible psychology. Mr. Herbert Spencer is
also in the same succession with a difference peculiar
to himself. It is a psychology which builds largely
on physiology, which explores the nervous system for
physical concomitants of psychological events, which
is great in the cross-examination of babies, and of late
years has dealt largely with the possible experiences
of the primitive man. It is great in the natural
history of man, especially in the growing period of
babyhood, youth, and early manhood. It is always
of opinion that a process of becoming explains the
result. Many other wonderful things might be said
of it. Alliance with evolution has not improved it,
but the alliance has enabled it to do more wonderful
things than ever. It has enabled Mr. Spencer to
suppose that he can manufacture intuitions, and
produce necessary principles as they are needed, and
to explain how what is *a priori* to the individual
may be *a posteriori* to the race. As if repetition,
custom, habit could ever generate a belief in principles
that are universal and necessary ! Prolong human
experience or life-experience as much as you please,
it is still a particular experience of the particular,

and it can never enable us to affirm a proposition as universal and necessary.

But perhaps the greatest feat ever performed in psychology is performed by Mr. Spencer when he affirms : " Not only do feelings constitute the inferior tracts of consciousness, but feelings are in all cases the materials out of which, in the superior tracts of consciousness, intellect is evolved by structural combination " (*Psychology*, vol. i., p. 192). That is something worth knowing ! Consciousness, Mr. Spencer repeatedly says, is built up of individual sensations and emotions. The simplest element of consciousness is compared to a nervous shock. Given a nervous shock, or repeated nervous shocks, and by combining and recombining these in endless ways consciousness is built up; for Mr. Spencer sensation and feeling are equivalent expressions. But, may we ask, what is it that is aware of the nervous shock ? Make feeling as simple as we may, before it becomes feeling, or when it becomes feeling there is a something which is aware of it. The lowest organism is one; it has a unitary centre somewhere, which reacts against the stimulus and the sensation. But Mr. Spencer deals with feelings as if they existed apart from a creature whose feelings they are. By a process of combining and recombining them he endeavours to build up a consciousness; but the consciousness is the condition of their existence. Feeling presupposes consciousness, and yet it is assumed that feeling makes consciousness.

Mr. Spencer speaks constantly of " relations between feelings," and he has not explained how this is possible.

Feeling is itself a relation between the object and the subject, and relations between feelings are just relations between the several objects and the one subject. With this understanding of the meaning of the relations between feelings, we can follow Mr. Spencer's exposition of the subject with interest and instruction. He has cast much light on the process of the coalescence of feelings into larger wholes; but he has not approached the goal he professedly has in view—that of enabling us to understand how consciousness is built up : "Clusters of clusters of feelings held together by relations of an extremely involved kind." Yes ; but the bond which holds them together is that they are referred to the conscious subject which holds them together in the unity of one self-consciousness.

But the one thing which English psychologists have ever sought to avoid is just this unity of self-consciousness. We get from them quite a number of useful observations. We get endless disquisitions on mind and body, on the nervous system and its psychological accompaniments, on the laws of association, on mental faculties, on the emotions and the will, and on a thousand other topics ; but they have so dealt with all of them as to make us forget that the feelings, emotions, volitions, associations belong to a self, are those of a self-conscious rational being. The self is lost amid the feelings, cognitions, and volitions ; and psychology proceeds as if these feelings, cognitions, and volitions were separate and independent realities. One might suppose that Professor Green, in his drastic and dramatic Introduction to Hume, had made an end of that kind of thing. But no : English psychology seems, like the Bourbons, to have learnt nothing and to have forgotten nothing. It is still alive, and has been recently reinforced from abroad, both from France and from Germany; and those who have recently dealt with the matter, Ribot and Münsterberg, have reduced consciousness to a mere accompaniment of physiological changes.

Notwithstanding this persistent view of psychology, and the reinforcement brought to it from beyond the sea, there is this to be said, that the presupposition of all possible psychology is the possibility of self-consciousness, to which all feelings, cognitions, volitions are to be referred. You may make of it what you please, but this much will remain, that it is the central unity to which all possible experience is to be referred. The self-conscious being stands over against all possible objects of experience, and refuses to be included among them. It is the self to which they are related, and in which the experience finds its unity.

It was necessary to say so much, in view of the attempt which is made to construct a natural history of the self. We have to admit that Dr. Romanes is aware of the problem, and that he says that in the work before us it is not the problem he has in hand. His is a problem of psychogenesis, and his aim is to prove that the intelligence of the man is not different in kind from that of the brute. We think he has failed; but his has been the most serious attempt that has been made, and the most valuable even to those who disagree with him. He has not made the attempt of building up mind from feelings as if they were independent realities. He knows that the organism is one connected whole, and that all the parts of an organism are mutually related in the unity of individual sensibility. "Every stimulus supplied from without, every movement originating from within, carries with it the character of belonging to that which feels or moves" (p. 197). Thus feelings are referred to their unifying centre; and he maintains also that thus the foundations of self-consciousness are largely laid in the fact that an organism is one connected whole. I do not myself see how this is consistent with the psychological pre-suppositions he derives from Locke. Dr. Romanes seems to assume that the only possible psychology is that of the empirical school. He is no doubt aware that the method and the conclusions of the empirical school are keenly contested. We now point only to Green's Introduction to Hume in witness of the fact. Dr. Romanes—for we must be brief—defines " idea " as follows : " The word 'idea' I will use in the sense defined in my previous work—namely, as a generic term to signify indifferently any product of imagination, from the mere memory of a sensuous impression up to the result of the most abstruse generalisation." Then he describes what he means by " simple idea," " complex idea," and " general idea." Then the different stages of ideation are given. Simple ideas he calls percepts, general ideas are concepts, and for the class which is between percepts and concepts he uses the word " recepts "; and he thinks that every one is likely to accept his classification. He thinks that in " perception " and in " reception " the mind is passive, while in " conceptual " thought it is active. We are not quite sure what to say about "recepts." They must either be particular, or they must be general. If they are more than particular, they must be representative; and if they are representative they are useless, and simply serve to perplex. But the question of the passivity of the mind until it reaches to general ideas is the most perplexing. It is this which we cannot reconcile with the statement of Dr. Romanes : " Every stimulus supplied from without, every movement originating from within, carries with it the character of belonging to that which feels and moves." If this be true, as we believe it is, then even in the lowest organism there is activity in response to stimulus. Much more is it true when a higher organism responds to stimulus. The activity may manifest itself even in feeling, and perception is activity. But this is not the only inconsistency into which Dr. Romanes has fallen "I take it, then, as established that true or conceptual self-consciousness consists in paying the same kind of attention to inward psychical consciousness as is habitually paid to outward psychical processes ; that in the mind of animals and infants there is a world of images standing as signs of outward objects, although we may concede that for the most part they only admit of being revived by sensuous association ; that at this stage of mental evolution the logic of recepts comprises an ejective as well as an objective world ; and that here we also have the recognition of individuality, so far as this is dependent on what has been termed an outward self-consciousness, or the consciousness of self as a feeling and an active agent, without the consciousness of self as an object of thought, and therefore a *subject* " (p. 200).

This is really a wonderful passage. We have read it again and again, and have read the passages which lead up to it, and those which immediately follow it, and with a wonder which grew and grew. What is the meaning of it ? I take note of the passage : " Receptual or outward self-consciousness is the practical recognition of self as an active and a feeling agent; while conceptual or inward self-consciousness is the introspective recognition of self as an object of knowledge, and therefore as a subject. Hence the one form of self-consciousness differs from the other in that it is only objective and never subjective." But that statement does not make the matter easier to understand. Does the higher self-consciousness never exist until it attains to the " recognition of itself as an object of knowledge " ? But the recognition of it does not make it. It is already there and active. Besides, Dr. Romanes would need to explain how the subject can become an object, how that for which all objects are, and to which all objects are presented, can be an object. That certain states of the subject can be an object can be readily understood, but not that the subject can be an object to itself. If the subject can be an object, how does it differ from other objects ? and what becomes of the distinction between the different forms of self-consciousness when the subject becomes an object ?

Then, again, what has the power or stage of conceptualism to do with the inward self-consciousness ? Have we no power to recognise ourselves as thinking, active, feeling beings until we have attained the stage of making concepts? or how do concepts help us to recognise ourselves? Is it that we must obtain the power of making and using general conceptions before we can recognise our own power of thinking? Is it that we can recognise the self as an object of knowledge only when we look at it under a general notion or idea? We submit in this case that the object of knowledge is not the self, but the general notion. This may perhaps be the meaning of Dr. Romanes, as it falls in with his psychological position generally. If it is, then psychology has again to pass through the period and the stages of controversy which have already been passed from Locke and Berkeley to Hume and his successors; and we shall have to discuss the question as to whether ideas are the only objects of knowledge. But that is a task which we may well decline.

At all events, Dr. Romanes has not made clear what he means by conceptual self-consciousness. Nor has he made good the distinction between outward and inner self consciousness; for after one attains to conceptual self-consciousness, he may live all his life and do all his work without ever turning his mind inward to contemplate itself. Dr. Romanes has himself the highest self-consciousness when he is occupied so completely with the study of external objects as to forget the inner self-consciousness altogether. Shall we say that Newton and Darwin and other great men, who hardly ever looked inward, but always outward, have not attained to the higher self-consciousness? That might be a plausible way of explaining some of the remarks of Darwin, and might help to explain why he thought of himself mainly as an object among other objects. But even that advantage will not tempt us to admit the precarious distinction which Dr. Romanes has drawn between outer and inner self-consciousness. The emergence of self-consciousness does not coincide with the emergence of the power of forming general concepts. Nor can we separate action and feeling from conception in that sharp and abrupt way. Activity and feeling are not separated from intelligence, and even the feeling of a self-conscious being is touched with rationality.

Now the interest of Dr. Romanes in this distinction arose from the fact that here for him is the dividing line between brutes and men. Following Locke, he makes the power of forming abstract ideas to belong only to man. "Therefore I think," says Locke, " beasts compare not their ideas further than some sensible circumstances annexed to the objects themselves. The other power of comparing, which may be observed in man, belonging to general ideas, and useful only in abstract reasonings, we may probably conjecture brutes have not." This is certainly a marked distinction between man and brutes, and Dr. Romanes has set it forth with admirable clearness. But is it psychologically the only distinction ? Does not the distinction between conscious and self-consciousness begin at an earlier stage ? Is it not manifested whenever the self is recognised as a feeling, acting, thinking agent ? Is not the self consciously there, even before the stage of introspection begins ?

To deny this is to deny self-consciousness to all who are not in the way of practising introspection, and this would involve the grotesque supposition that all our scientific men—our physicists, chemists, biologists, whose main work is to study facts and laws in their objective order, without reference to themselves as subjects—are destitute of the higher self-consciousness.

Apart, however, from any controversy about the stage when self-consciousness begins to manifest itself, let us accept Dr. Romanes' view that there is such a thing as self-consciousness. However we may understand the word, yet the fact that self-consciousness makes a distinction between man and brute is important. It serves to mark the position of man as unique. The recognition of self as an active, feeling, or, as Dr. Romanes says, as a thinking agent separates man from the whole lower world. Can we call this a distinction in kind? or is it only in degree? We shall not quarrel about the phrase, if we get the thing. We say it is a great distinction, call it as we please. It does not seem possible to explain it by anything but itself. We may say that " the foundations are laid in the fact that the organism is one connected whole "; but so we might say that the foundations of water are laid in oxygen and hydrogen, and the foundations of life are laid in the chemical properties of matter, but water and life have properties which cannot be explained by the characteristics of the foundations. So it appears to be with self-consciousness. It is unique; there is nothing like it in the world beneath; and as far as evolution is concerned, it is just bound to accept it, and to accept it without explanation.

Whatever the explanation may be, it must fulfil certain conditions. It must be such as will not break up the unity of human nature, and assign the origin of his body to one set of causes and his mind to another ; and it must not bring in a cause here which operates only at this point or at a few other points in the whole history of the earth. This is, however, what Mr. Russel Wallace has done, and the result is that he has advocated a certain kind of deism, as, in fact, Mr. Darwin has also. But deism is a super-annuated form of thought which cannot be resuscitated at the present hour. Mr. Wallace tells us that " there are at least three stages in the development of the organic world when some new cause or power must necessarily come into action. The first stage is the change from organic to inorganic, when the first vegetable cell, or the living protoplasm out of which it arose, first appeared. . . . The next stage is still more marvellous, still more completely beyond all possibility of explanation by matter, its laws, and forces. It is the introduction of sensation or conscious-ness, constituting the fundamental distinction between the animal and vegetable kingdoms. . . . The third stage is, as we have seen, the existence in man of a number of his most characteristic and noblest faculties, those which raise him furthest above the brutes, and open up possibilities of almost indefinite advancement. These faculties could not possibly have been developed by means of the same laws which have determined the progressive development of the organic world in general, and also of man's physical organism. These three distinct stages of progress

from the inorganic world of matter up to man point
clearly to an unseen universe, to a world of spirit, to
which the world of matter is altogether subordinate."
(*Darwinism*, pp. 274-6.)

These are the positions, this is the attitude of
mind which we call deistic, and which, on grounds of
science, philosophy, and theology, we cannot accept.
Are we to hold that only at these three stages can we
find anything that points to a world of spirit? Are
we to bring in the world of spirit only where our
favourite theory fails? If there are breaks like these
in the theory of evolution, is it not time to revise our
theory? For if it cannot explain these points of new
departure, it cannot really explain anything? It is
curious to notice how the deistic view has got itself
wrought into the very structure of Mr. Wallace's
mind. "The theory of 'continual interference' is a
limitation of the Creator's power. It assumes that he
could not work by pure law in the organic as he has
done in the inorganic world; it assumes that he could
not foresee the consequences of the laws of matter and
mind combined—that results would continually arise
which are contrary to what is best, and that he has
to change what would otherwise be the order of
nature, in order to produce that beauty and variety
and harmony which even we, with our limited intel-
lects, can conceive to be the result of self-adjustment
in a universe governed by unvarying law." (*Natural
Selection*, p. 240.) Is there no way of conceiving the
action of the Divine presence and power in the world
save that of continual interference? Why should we
with Mr. Wallace postulate the absence of God from

the world save only at these critical points where the
self-adjusting forces had failed and were unequal to
the new departure? Having made the new departure
Mr. Wallace thinks that, having got such a start, the
world could again be left to self-adjusting, self-acting
laws. Might it not help Mr. Wallace if he were to
read Butler, and learn from him that the laws of
nature are just the uniform action of God? It is not
possible to think that God is ever absent from His
creation, or we must think that He is always absent.
Theology cannot accept a mere *deus ex machina*.

Nor can we accept that view of Mr. Wallace which
asserts one origin for man's physical organism and
another for his spiritual nature. Such a view destroys
the unity of man, and simply makes him a highly
organised animal to which somehow a spiritual
nature has been superadded. It is surrounded with
difficulties. Man proceeds by ordinary generation ;
how has this superadded spiritual nature been transmitted? Man has a true body and a reasonable
soul; is each reasonable soul superadded to each individual as he comes into existence? Is it not more
reasonable, as it is certainly more Scriptural, to trace
the origin of man, body, soul, spirit, as a unity, to
the creative power of God? Certainly the Scripture
teaches that in the future, in another life, man in
his complete state will be an organic man, with a
spiritual body adequate to express his spiritual
nature. Are we, then, to deny even in the case of
man " special creation "? Yes and no, as we understand the meaning of the term. To me creation is
continuous. To me everything is as it is through the

continuous power of God; every law, every being, every relation of being are determined by Him, and He is the Power by which all things exist. I believe in the immanence of God in the world, and I do not believe that He comes forth merely at a crisis, as Mr. Wallace supposes. Apart from the Divine action man would not have been, or have an existence ; but apart from the Divine action nothing else would have an existence.

We have seen, with the help of Dr. Romanes, that the self-conscious man is a unique being in the world, that there is none like him. Are we to think also that this is a lonely kind of existence in this universe or above this universe ? He is a being who can look before and after, who can think, and conceive the order and method and evolution of the universe; and he can gather up the wealth of his experience into the unity of his self-consciousness. Is there any other being like him, a Being in whose image he is, who can speak to him, and to whom he can speak ? Man has been able to look back on a world which was once without life. But even in that world he was able to recognise power, regulated power, which proceeded rationally in a manner which can be understood by man : power in the systems of the stars, power in the solar system, power in the early history of the lifeless earth; not a random power, but a power that worked by law, by method, and in order. He saw that the power he recognised proceeded stage by stage until a world was made with conditions fit for life. Is he wrong if he thinks that the power manifested in the living world was a power to which life was

no stranger? that the power was a living power? Is
he wrong in thinking that the power he knows in
the living world as living, now that self-consciousness
has appeared, is not lacking in this respect? Is he
not right in thinking that this power has in itself
all the endowments which have been manifested one
after another in the world of life, intelligence, self-
consciousness? And it has these eternally. We
know that power, life, consciousness, self-consciousness
arose one after another, and we may be greatly exercised about the method and manner of their appearance. But will not the perplexity be greatly lessened
if we have reason to believe in a Power, living, intelligent, self-conscious, to whose creative energy and
eternal wisdom all things owe their being and their
character? But this is to postulate an eternal Self-
consciousness. Yes; and why not? It is a more
reasonable assumption than the assumption of an
eternal unconsciousness, out of which, in the process
of the ages, a self-consciousness should arise.

CHAPTER X

EVOLUTION AND ETHICS

Ethics of evolution—Professor Huxley's ethical ideal—
Whence derived?—Not from cosmic process, not from
Greek or Roman ethics, nor from ordinary human ethics
—Ethical life : what it is—Struggle for existence partial
in cosmos ; at its fiercest in human life—Spheres of
human conduct non-moralised—Moral ideals—Moral
obligation—The Christian ethical ideal—Its acknowledged supremacy—Its character—Recognition of it—
Not derived from evolution—Christian ethics both Test
and Goal of ethical evolution.

WITH the advent of a self-conscious being into
the world, the world has taken on a new
meaning.   Here is a being who can stand over
against the world, oppose himself to it, who can say
" I," and distinguish himself from everything else.
The change thus made in the universe is of unspeak-
able importance; for here is a being who can, in
course of time, become the greatest factor in the
cosmos, can read the process of its becoming, and
forecast in a measure its final outcome.   He is part
of the process; but in so far as he can oppose himself
to it he is greater than it, and can in a measure
control it.   So far as we can limit our view of man
to the intellectual side, and regard him mainly as a
rational, self-conscious being, we are able to say that

he is an immeasurable advance on all that has gone
before. All the intelligence formally manifested in
the cosmos, so far as consciousness has gone, is only
rudimentary. It is when we come to look at the
moral and social life of man that the strangest
phenomena appear. It is not our purpose here to
trace the history of the phenomena of ethics, or to
criticise the attempts that have been made to bring
them into line with the theory of evolution. We
have many such attempts. Mr. Spencer, Mr. Leslie
Stephen, Mr. Darwin, and others have sought to
trace the evolution of ethics. We have also many
contributions from the students of anthropology. A
full and critical account may be found in the work
of Mr. C. M. Williams, *A Review of the Systems of
Ethics founded on the Theory of Evolution*, who, after
giving us a valuable account of the systems of ethics
founded on evolution, himself adds one to the number.
Of all of them it may be said generally that the
explanation they give of the phenomena of the moral
life is inadequate, and these phenomena are for the
most part explained away.

That evolution is not inconsistent with the recognition of moral ideals we may see by a reference to
the system of Mr. Spencer. We may see this also
by a reference to the latest and the most remarkable
of the writings of Professor Huxley. A great part
of the Romanes lecture (*Evolution and Ethics*) is of
such a kind as to make us inclined to forget many
of the fierce and bitter things which the Professor
has written in the course of his most controversial
life. "As I have already said, the practice of

that which is ethically best—what we call goodness or virtue—involves a course of conduct which, in all respects, is opposed to that which leads to success in the cosmic struggle for existence. In place of ruthless self-assertion, it demands self-restraint; in place of thrusting aside or treading down all competitors, it requires that the individual shall not merely respect, but shall help his fellows; its influence is directed, not so much to the survival of the fittest, as to the fitting of as many as possible to survive. It repudiates the gladiatorial theory of existence. It demands that each man who enters into the enjoyments of a polity shall be mindful of his debt to those who have laboriously constructed it, and shall take heed that no act of his weakens the fabric in which he has been permitted to live. Laws and moral precepts are directed to the end of curbing the cosmic process, and reminding the individual of his duty to the community, to the protection and influence of which he owes, if not existence itself, at least the life of something better than a brutal savage." (*Ethics and Evolution,* pp. 33, 34.) "Let us understand, once for all, that the ethical progress of society depends, not in imitating the cosmic process, still less in running away from it, but in combating it." Here Professor Huxley sets forth an ethical ideal of a noble order. From what source has he derived it ?

It is not from the cosmic process. Nor has he found it in the ethical systems he has passed in review in the previous part of his lecture. It coincides in a large degree with the ethics of the Sermon on the Mount; and we may be glad that Professor Huxley agrees with it ; not so much for the sake of the Sermon on the Mount as for his own sake. We are not sure, however, as to whether on his own principles Professor Huxley has a right to separate the ethical from the cosmic process. On what ground does he justify his moral ideal ? We hardly know. We are too glad, however, to have these noble words of his with respect to the moral ideal to inquire too curiously into its sources and its sanction.

At the same time, we feel bound to ask whether the cosmic process is what Professor Huxley has described it to be, or whether it is not a kind of anthropomorphism, whether it is not a reading of man's practices into the cosmos. The struggle for existence has been made to play a great part in the theory of evolution. Is it not exaggerated ? In fact, the typical form of the struggle for existence is not cosmic, but human, and has its most perfect expression in the science of political economy as that science has been formerly expounded. In it self-interest is regarded as the ruling motive, and from it as a motive, with the fact of private property and freedom of competition, the laws of the science are formulated. Unlimited freedom of competition, baker against baker, draper against draper, company against company, shipowner against shipowner, and one class against another,—thus we have the struggle for existence in its highest form.

As we go back in history we find that the struggle for existence which we see to-day pressed most keenly in the industrial form has had other ways of manifesting itself in the world of man. There is war, and the development of the warlike spirit. There is the hostility between tribe and tribe, between city and city, between kingdom and kingdom. From the beginning of recorded history until now what Professor Huxley has called the cosmic process has been more fully realised in the world of man than in the lower world. From one point of view it looks as if the gift of self-conscious life, the power of reflection and of conscious adaptation of means to ends, were not a boon; for on the stage of history the self-conscious being has largely shown himself to be a being of the most selfish sort. " Man the animal," says Professor Huxley, " in fact, has worked his way to the headship of the sentient world, and has become the superb animal he is, in virtue of his success in the struggle for existence. The conditions having been of a certain order, man's organisation has adjusted itself to them better than that of his competitors in the cosmic strife. In the case of mankind, the self-assertion, the unscrupulous seizing upon all that can be grasped, the tenacious holding of all that can be kept, which constitute the essence of the struggle for existence, have answered. For his successful progress as far as the savage state man has been largely indebted to those qualities which he shares with the ape and the tiger: his exceptional physical organisation; his cunning, his sociability, his curiosity, and his imitativeness; his ruthless and ferocious destructiveness when his anger is roused by opposition." (Pp. 5, 6.)

Thus the appearance of a self-conscious, rational being on the stage of life served only to accentuate

and to intensify the struggle for existence. It is a
striking and an appalling fact, which would seem to
require a more radical examination and a deeper
explanation than that given to it by Professor Huxley;
for from this point of view man is something worse
than the lower world. He has fallen from the level
of the higher animals, and reason in him has been
pressed into the service of selfishness, ruthlessness,
and ferocity; and the nature which is higher from
an intellectual point of view has, ethically regarded,
become lower. This fact would need to be explained,
and theology has an explanation, on which I do not
insist at present. The matter now in hand is to
press home the fact that the Darwinian notion of the
struggle for existence has been derived, not from the
cosmos, but from the more virulent form of human
competition; and if our thinking is to correspond to
fact, we must make allowance for the exaggeration;
for the presence of reason, uncontrolled by conscience
and unguided by moral considerations, serves only to
make the possessor of it more selfish, and more powerful in his self-assertion. He has got into possession
of the most powerful of all instruments, and he uses
it without remorse for selfish ends. If a rational
being allows himself to be selfish, then he becomes
more intensely selfish than any other being of a
lower order. The desires of an ape and a tiger are
limited: if they can get sufficient food for the day
they are content for the day, and the struggle is only
for the day. The desires of a rational being are
practically unlimited, and every object may become
an object of desire. The competition between him

and his fellows is practically unlimited, and the struggle for existence has no ending.

The cosmic struggle for existence is therefore partial and limited. It is neither so fierce nor so persistent as is represented. It is modified also by co-operation, and by many instances of mutual help and benefit. There is the adumbration of self-sacrifice in the lower world, though there it is in the region of instinct, and not in that of conscious reflection and purpose. The individual sacrifices itself for the species; and as the species ascend in rank, the sacrifice becomes greater and greater, until among them there is something like the appearance of family life. Then we find such cases as are manifested in a law of mutual helpfulness impressed on very different kinds for the advantage of each. Instances might readily be enumerated, and more and more of these beneficial inter-relations are being discovered every day.

We are therefore driven to the conclusion that the process against which ethics has to strive is not so much a cosmic as it is a human process. For we do find in the cosmic process the outlines and the rudiments of that ethical doctrine set forth so eloquently by Professor Huxley. We find the law of self-sacrifice at work in the grain, and in the flower. We find the law of social unity adumbrated in the vine and its branches. We find the outline of a settled social state in the community of the ant and the bee, where each individual works not for its own benefit, but for the benefit of the community. And in many other instances also we have involuntary foreshadowings of the ethical ideal.

Ethically the problem to be solved is, How is it that in man we have the curious result of both the fiercest insistence on the unethical cosmic process and the most strenuous insistence on the necessity of combating it? It affords no solution of the problem to say that man the animal has worked his way up in virtue of his success in the struggle for existence; for we have no evidence that man the mere animal ever existed. And if he ever were only an animal, he would not have persisted or survived in the struggle for existence. A rational, self-conscious being ought, as such, to have a moral consciousness and a rational order in his moral life. As a matter of fact, we see that there have been rational beings who really seem to fight not against what Professor Huxley calls the cosmic process, but against the moral order. They have exaggerated all the selfish elements of the cosmic process, and have become superbly selfish.

Nor can we solve the problem by saying that this phase of development belongs to the time before men passed from anarchy to civilisation. As a matter of fact, the gladiatorial theory of existence was never more in vogue than it is in the present hour. We see it in the field of international relations, nations armed to the throat, and each nation adding to its army because its neighbour has made some movement of the same kind. There are about twenty millions of men in arms in Europe at the present hour; ships are built; and the talk everywhere is not of duty, not of principle, but of self-interest. Nor does a different state of things meet our view in the industrial world. In truth, over a wide field of human activity we find that men are not combating the cosmic process, but are imitating it, and are improving on the pattern, and the cosmic process by becoming rational has become ethically worse. Nor is this the worst; for the problem is not merely that of the difference between men and men: it is the difference within the same man. All the week through men live according to the cosmic process, and on Sunday they profess to believe a religion, one main feature of which is set forth in the Sermon on the Mount. On Monday they buy in the cheapest and sell in the dearest market, and feel that their conduct is sanctioned by the purest laws of political economy, and all the while they profess to believe that he who saves his life shall lose it, and he that loses his life shall save it.

From the point of view of evolution as manifested in the cosmic process, we have no criterion of right or wrong, nor of good and evil; for it is the fittest that survive, and the survival proves the fitness. We are not helped by the criterion of Mr. Spencer that right conduct is the conduct that is most evolved. The immoral sentiments are as evolved as the moral. There is a great deal of definite, coherent heterogeneity in the burglar and the thief. And the conduct of the first Napoleon exhibits a great example of evolved conduct; but his ethical character does not rise to the standard set by Professor Huxley. In fact, as the conditions of society get more and more complex, and the struggle for existence becomes more and more keen, conduct, whether it is good or bad, necessarily becomes more evolved. Selfishness must become more cunning, and must adapt itself to the conditions of existence.

It seems necessary to lay stress on this sad fact of our common humanity, as it is an aspect of human life too much neglected in systematic ethical treatises. Why has man been, why *is* man so unethical? It is a pleasant exercise for ethical writers to trace the origin and progress of the ethical emotions, to show us the first faint traces of sympathy, self-sacrifice, and love in the lower creation, to point us to the evolution of motherhood and the growth of family life, to show us the first growth of moral maxims, and their increase in complexity and simplicity, until we get to the moral code of to-day. But it might be well if they traced also the history of the dark shadow that has hung over human life from the beginning, and try to understand and explain it; for side by side with the evolution of good conduct there has gone the evolution of evil conduct; and we cannot account for this on the ground of any mere evolutionary process. Even if we could trace the progress of evolved morality, that will hardly give us a criterion of good conduct; and we must obtain an explanation from some other source.

It seems a difficult task to account for the existence of a moral ideal on the part of man when we look at him as a product of the cosmic process. It seems difficult, when we look at the current maxims of conduct, to understand how or where Professor Huxley has got his ethical ideal; for the maxims of common conduct, such as business is business, England must pursue her career and look after her interests, and other maxims which in business life and national life make self-interest the ruling motive, are quite opposed to his high ideal. The two ideals are really inconsistent ; and it seems scarcely possible to account for the existence of moral ideals, of the kind set forth by Professor Huxley, as an unaided achievement of the human mind, or as the outcome of an evolutionary process. For men are worse than they ought to be, considered as products of evolution, and men are also better ; and both in their badness and in their goodness they seem to transcend the cosmic order.

In this connection it might be well to consider the character of moral ideals, of moral institutions, and of the moral sphere ; for as a matter of history moral ideals have changed from age to age, and moral institutions and moral enactments have also varied, while the strange thing with regard to morals is the vast extent of human activity which seems to lie outside of man's moral regard. Stress has been laid by writers on the fact of obligation, and the moral feeling implied in the words " ought " and " duty." All are agreed that these are words which represent ethical facts of the highest importance. Various explanations are given both of the origin of them, their character, and their sanctions ; but whatever these may be, there is agreement as to the fact that man somehow feels himself bound to aim at a moral life. We accept the fact, then, of moral coerciveness ; but the fact does not explain the differences in the moral ideal which have appeared in the course of history between man and man, between one generation and another, and between nation and nation. Have we not one ideal in India, another in Persia, another in

Greece, another in Rome? and to-day have we not different ideals in modern life, and in modern nations?

The obligation to do right, the feeling of "ought" may be universal in man, as we do not doubt it is; but how is a man to know what the moral ideal is, and how is it to be embodied in his own life and in social life? One thing is sure, that when we look at the contemporary life of to-day we find large tracts of it which seem to lie outside of ethical action properly regarded. How small is the sphere in which duty appears to rule! While the feeling of obligation is existent in every man, yet how narrow is its scope! It does not seem to reach beyond a few conventional moralities. Hardly any one makes the whole of his life an expression of goodwill and right reason. Indifference to one's own health, intemperance in food and drink, abiding in ignorance when knowledge can be attained,—these are as common as possible, and are scarcely ever visited with the disapproval which they merit. Neglect of means which are needed to save life, whether these be the observance of sanitary laws, or the proper precautions in order that work may be carried on in safety, and a hundred other neglects of the same order, which issue in the ill health and death of many, are scarcely looked at as wrong at all. Then there is scarcely any recognition of public duty, and often a man who is sensitively conscientious in the discharge of personal duty feels no responsibility and takes no action in public matters; or if he takes action he simply votes with his party. It is evident, therefore, that there is a large sphere of human action into which the thought of duty and responsibility has not yet penetrated, nor will it penetrate until we learn that the social order is the only thing which makes individual growth in a moral life possible, and if there is a low tone of public morality a high-toned and moral life is scarcely possible.

Then, again, we have a formal claim set up, that various human activities should proceed on their own lines unhampered and unhindered by ethical considerations. It is scarcely possible to enumerate these, so many have they been. Art has claimed that it has a right to neglect morality, and to cultivate the beautiful for its own sake. Literature also has had its fleshly school and its realisms, which have not lacked defenders at the present hour. Trade and commerce make their claim that they have a right to pursue their own end in their own way. Politics also has become, or perhaps has always been, on a non-moral basis, and party-spirit is sometimes so keen that the facts can scarcely be seen in the mists of controversy. A wide survey of the life of to-day leads to the conclusion that the field of ethical action is circumscribed to a strange degree. But it is evident that if ethics is the art of true living—of ideal living, shall we say?—then the ethical rules must be universal, and no human activity can be left outside its scope.

The shifting moral ideals of the past, and the utter imperfection of moral institutions, as also the slight extent to which human life has been moralised, all tend to show us that the ethical ideal set forth by Professor Huxley must have some other source than that of mere human evolution. The ethical ideal already quoted by him is, in some respects, identical with that of the Sermon on the Mount and of the New Testament generally. How different this ethics was from contemporary ethics any one knows who has given any attention to the subject. How different was the view of the sacredness of human life in Christian and in non-Christian ethics! Plato allowed infanticide as fitting in certain circumstances, and Aristotle viewed slavery as founded in the very nature of things; but the New Testament taught that God had made of one blood all the nations of the earth, and looked on all men as alike partakers of one human nature, and therefore all alike entitled to equal justice. From the unity of human nature, from the greatness of human destiny and from a universal Divine redemption, conclusions were drawn which contained in them implicitly the reversal of many ethical judgments, and set forth an ideal utterly subversive of a large amount of current practice. There is no ethical ideal like the ideal of Jesus of Nazareth, realised in His own life and set forth in His teaching.

It seems a hard thing to say that this moral ideal has never been sufficiently understood, or really and seriously taken. Dr. Hatch says: "The ethics of the Sermon on the Mount, which the earliest Christian communities endeavoured to carry into practice, have been transmuted by the slow alchemy of history into the ethics of Roman law. The basis of Christian society is not Christian, but Roman and Stoical. A portion of the Roman conception of rights with the

Stoical conception of relations involving reciprocal actions is in possession of practically the whole field of civilised society. The transmutation is so complete that the modern question is not so much whether the ethics of the Sermon on the Mount are practicable, as whether, if practicable, they would be desirable." (*Hibbert Lectures*, pp. 169, 170.) It would be well, then, to go back to the Sermon on the Mount, to the life and conduct and teaching of Jesus of Nazareth, and to try in the first place to understand these. To know plainly what these mean, apart from all questions as to whether these precepts of His are practicable and desirable, apart also from all questions as to their origin and tendency, would seem to be one of the first duties of this generation. For the study of them has been hindered in many ways—hindered by prejudice and preconceptions, by our bringing with us to the study of them conceptions derived from Roman and Stoic sources, and by current ethical conceptions of a kind similar to the prevailing ideas of Greek ethics. As to the interpretation of Christ's moral precepts, there have been discussions as to whether they really mean what they seem to mean, and for the most part they are interpreted to mean something else. It seems to be held that His words have something rash about them, that they are stated too absolutely, that they need to be toned down, guarded, attenuated in some way, until they are brought more in accordance with man's usual judgments. Even Christian commentators seem somehow to lose courage in the presence of these broad, strong, ethical judgments of Jesus Christ ; as a consequence, the breadth and universality and unconditional character of His teaching have been obscured, and even the people who profess to follow Him hardly ever get face to face with the moral ideal of Jesus Christ without a veil between.

If this be largely so with regard to the understanding of His teaching, much more is it so with regard to the practice of it.   No one, or but very few have had the courage even to try to obey the commands of Christ.   Certainly no nation has tried to do so.   In fact, some Christian teachers have distinctly said that it is not the duty of nations to obey the precepts of the Sermon on the Mount.   It may be acknowledged that we are far from the time when men or nations are likely seriously to try this way of life.   Certainly men will never seriously try it as long as the present attitude of mind towards that teaching is maintained.   As long as that teaching is not taken seriously, as long as its commands are looked at as mere counsels of perfection, so long will the present lack of effort continue.   Were, however, the teaching of Christ and His example taken as true, and binding, and authoritative, and were the kind of moral life inculcated by Him taken as the only kind of life fit for men to live, what a different kind of world this world would become !   If self-assertion were to pass out of existence, and poverty of spirit take its place ; if the hunger and thirst after righteousness were to become as insistent, peremptory, and imperative as the hunger and thirst after food and drink for the body, and as imperiously demanded satisfaction ; if the purity of heart that can see God were to become common, and the peacemakers become as universal as man, is there any one who can

13

doubt that the things which now mar our peace and trouble the prospects of humanity would speedily pass away? No one can doubt that, if the ethical ideal of Jesus Christ were to be universally realised, we should have a world wherein righteousness would reign; and this can be said of no other ethical ideal.

It is a commonplace to say that He is the only moral Teacher who ever realised His own ideal. What He taught He lived, and what He commanded others to do He first realised in His own conduct. In this there is a great contrast; for whatever' a man's moral ideal is, it may be safely said that his practice comes short of it. Take a man wherever you may find him, in ancient Greece, Rome, Persia, Egypt, and you find in him a difference between the ideal life and the·real, the life he feels he ought to live and the life he actually does live. It is in this connection that the fact of moral obligation has its unique place. Universally man's conception of duty is higher than he can realise. The "ought" is always greater than the reality. *Video proboque meliora deteriora sequor* is an old saying universally recognised as true. It is so when the ideal of moral life has not been wide, or deep, or high; much more so, as the moral ideal becomes higher, and as wider experience reveals the infinite character of duty. The discrepancy between the ideal and the real, between what ought to be and what is, is largely present to the mind of every one. The man of greatest attainments feels it most keenly, and his sorrow at the fact is sometimes too deep for expression.

That the ethical ideal of human life set forth in the

New Testament is the highest, purest, best, is a proposition which is almost universally recognised as true. It has become the standard by which all other ethical standards are measured and judged. It has found its way in whole or in part into almost every system of ethics, and the greatest task which ethical students have is to find a way by which the ethical ideal of Christianity can be brought into their systems and harmonised with their leading principles. The religion of humanity has given the new ethical principle the name of Altruism; Mr. Herbert Spencer recognises it, and is disposed to complain that his scientific basis for morals has been anticipated by the ethical principles of Christianity; for the Hegelians the principle of self-sacrifice has become the central principle of their philosophy and religion; and Kant's leading rules of ethics are but the abstract form of what was concretely set forth in the New Testament. It is not too much to say that the life and teaching of Jesus Christ have penetrated to the very centre of our modern theory in ethics, that they have moulded the thoughts and influenced the judgment of the greatest writers on ethics, and have given endless trouble to them; for they must make the ethical conception of Christianity square in some measure at least with their fundamental ideas.

Büchner tells us that " our present state of culture has already long since left behind it all, and even the highest, intellectual ideals elaborated by former religions. The only correct, tenable moral principle depends on the relation of reciprocity. There is therefore no better guide to moral conduct than the old and well-known proverb, 'What ye would not have done to you that to others never do.' If we complete the proverb with the addition, ' Do to others as ye would that they should do to you,' we have the entire code of virtue and morals, and indeed in a better and simpler form than could be furnished by the thickest manuals of ethics, or the quintessence of all the religious systems of the world." When Comte sought to condense his ethical system into a sentence he wrote, " It is more blessed to give than to receive " ; but this last sentence, which contains the essence of positivist ethics, is already familiar to readers of the New Testament : " Ye ought to help the weak, and to remember the words of the Lord Jesus, how He Himself said, It is more blessed to give than to receive " (Acts xx. 35). The entire code of ethics according to Büchner is already found in the Sermon on the Mount : " All things therefore whatsoever ye would that men should do unto you, even so do ye also unto them : for this is the law and the prophets " (Matt. vii. 12).

Nor do we find any advance on the ideal of Christian ethics in those maxims formulated by Kant, of which it has been said that they occupy a place in ethics corresponding to the place which the three laws of motion have in the physical sciences : " (1) Act so that the maxim of thy will may be capable of being a universal law ; (2) act so that thou mayest use the humanity in thy own person, as well as in the person of every other, always as an end, and never as a means ; (3) act according to maxims which at the same time may be objectified as natural laws in a system of universal legislation." These are but the abstract expression of the commonplaces of Christian ethics. The first maxim asks us to look at each individual act in the light of a universal law. What would be the result if every one acted so? We may say of the second that it could scarcely have been formulated had not Christianity paved the way, and if the Christian view of human life had not obtained recognition. It simply says that a man must remain a man, must not allow himself to become a mere tradesman, engineer, politician, orator, or man of science. He must be a man with all humanity in himself, and must not make of himself or of others a means to an end. How readily we may use ourselves as means to an end need hardly be said. No better illustration of this can be given than Darwin himself. How readily also we use other people merely as means! How easily we make a man an abstraction, look at him only in one aspect, and that the aspect of him which we can most easily use! Soldiers for a general are not men, but only so much fighting power, which has to be kept in good order, and fit to be in a certain place at a certain time to do certain work; for the capitalist men are so much labour; for the merchant men are so many customers; and generally we are all looked on by ourselves and others as means to an end. In the third Kant asks, Would our maxims, if acted on, maintain the moral order of the universe? or would they throw the moral universe into confusion, and let us judge accordingly?

But the maxims of Kant are really different forms of the teaching of Christ, and apart from the ethical spirit of Christ would remain barren abstractions. Christ embodied these maxims in a concrete life; of Him alone could it be said that He always acted so, as described in Kant's maxims. The basis of His actions might at any moment be made universal, and at any moment might adequately be made natural laws in a system of universal legislation. He was the first, as He is indeed the only one who taught the infinite worth of man. Institutions were made for man, not man for institutions. He alone saw the height and depth and possibilities of humanity, and He alone was able to penetrate beyond the differences between races, nations, tribes, individuals, classes, and discern the common human nature. He saw men in the light of eternity, and thus He taught that all things are for men, and man for God.

The ethical ideal set up by Christ, though imperfectly understood and only partially realised in His followers, has obtained the victory. To be like Christ, to live as He lived, to resolve that not pleasure but service shall be the guide of life, that not self-indulgence, but self-denial, self-sacrifice for great and worthy ends shall be our motive, this is the ideal of life which has won the approval of the best and noblest of men. "We needs must love the highest when we know it." And that Christ's ethical ideal is the highest is almost universally recognised.

What is the bearing of these things on the ethics of evolution, or on the evolution of ethics? Well, this much at least is implied: that at a certain period in the world's history a certain ethical ideal arose, was embodied in the life and conduct of its Founder, and set forth in His teaching ; an ethical ideal which was to win slowly, and in the face of stern opposition, such approval for itself, that by the more advanced people it shall be recognised as the best and highest for man. It looks as if it had not been evolved *by* man, but evolved *for* man ; an ideal of true living which he did not form for himself, but which he could recognise as right and true and good when it was set before him. It could scarcely have been formed by man, since it reversed his usual ethical judgments, disapproved what he had approved, and approved what he disapproved. What is evolved must always bear some relation to the process of evolution and to the lines on which evolution proceeded.

This conclusion becomes even more stringent when we consider not only the ethical ideals before Christ, but the ethical ideals since His ideal has been before men. His ethical ideal cannot be placed in the line of evolution. It stands out from all others, distinct in character and aim, in promise and in fulfilment. It, unlike all other ethical speculations, has not taken its place as a mere factor in ethical theory which subsequent speculation has absorbed and transcended. We can write a history of the evolution of ethics, and can show something like relation between one stage and another in every case except that of Christ. Some relation and preparation there are between before and after, save only here. But in this case a moral ideal appears, which does not merely become a platform for further devolopment, which is not appropriated and transcended, which is largely misunderstood, and not acted on, which even to the present hour remains an unapproachable standard of ideal moral life, something which tests all other moral ideals, and is itself beyond all tests. Evolution can deal with such a problem in only two ways : it must either show that the moral ideal of Christianity is just what we ought to expect in the time and place and circumstances of its origin, and that its origin and character are not exceptional ; or it must show that it is not of a kind fitted to be the highest ideal of humanity in every age and time. Either task seems impossible. For Jesus Christ as a moral Person, as a moral Influence, and as a moral Teacher infinitely transcends, not only the men of His own time, but the men of every time ; and the testimony of our best ethical writers bears witness to the worth and value of the Christian ideal of life.

In the Christian view of God and of His relation to the world such an event as depicted is not unintelligible. It means that the processes, laws, and operations of the world have not proceeded apart from God. It means that God was making the world for a purpose, and that He guided and ruled it by laws appropriate to the nature of the things He has made ; that each higher grade of being manifests more clearly and fully the nature of " the infinite and eternal Energy from which all things proceed." It means also that the infinite and eternal Energy not only manifests Himself in the world, but manifests Himself *to* the world as soon as there is a world capable of apprehending the manifestation. Thus, when by the slow processes of His creative power and wisdom He had made a creature rational and self-conscious, He began to manifest Himself to him in ways he could apprehend. There is here also a process of slow growth and evolution. " That is not first which is spiritual, but that which is natural, then that which is spiritual." It may take a long time and much toil to make that which is spiritual ; but God is never absent from His creation, and never ceases to be in living contact with it. We proceed on the assumption that God is something for Himself.

Let us say, with Mr. Spencer, " that the power manifested throughout the universe distinguished as material is the same power which in ourselves wells up under the form of consciousness." Have we any other affirmation to make of that power ? Mr. Spencer himself distinguished between the power and its manifestations, though his distinction is that the power is unknowable, while the manifestation may be known. It might be more logical to say that the power is known by its manifestations. May we not, however, logically say that the power manifested within consciousness and throughout the universe is not exhausted by these manifestations—that the power is something for itself, and if so may be manifested in some other ways ? Why may not that power manifest itself *to* man in some way which could not be accomplished either by welling up in consciousness or by action in the material universe ? Mr. Spencer dismisses as incredible the thought that "the cause to which we can put no limit in space or time, and of which our entire solar system is a relatively infinitesimal product, took the disguise of a man for the purpose of covenanting with a shepherd chief in

Syria" (*Principles of Sociology,* "Ecclesiastical Institutions," p. 704). Exception might be taken to the terms of the statement, but, waiving that, we look to the merely quantitative terms of the comparison. What if Abraham were of more value than the whole material of the solar system? What if the self-conscious, ethical, spiritual life of man were the end for which the solar system is? What if the proposition which Mr. Spencer dismisses as incredible were to be justified by his own example? He has devoted a lifetime to the production of the Synthetic Philosophy. From the outset he has had in view the purpose of providing a scientific basis for ethics and a scientific guide to conduct. He is fond of speaking of the naturally revealed end to which evolution tends. We cannot suppose that the Power which works through evolution is indifferent to the end in view. Why should not the Power, "of which the entire solar system is a relatively infinitesimal product," reveal Himself to Abraham, if by that revelation He could bring about that ethical life which is the goal of evolution, as that goal is shadowed forth in Mr. Spencer's works? Did Mr. Spencer hope to influence moral conduct by his laborious life and by the results of his thought and toil? Is he to deny to the Power of which he is himself a product the capacity of doing what he has himself done? Then there is something in Mr. Spencer unaccounted for by the Power of which he is a product? If Mr. Spencer can speak to his fellow-men, and seek to influence them to the pursuit of high and noble ends, why should not the Power which wells up in his consciousness have the same privilege? If the end to which evolution tends is worthy, then the Power which manifests itself in evolution may take direct means to effect that end. It is but a manifestation of that Power in a form suited to the end in view, and to the nature of the being to whom it is manifested. We submit that what is possible to Mr. Spencer is possible to God; and if the production of moral life is a worthy outcome of the toil manifested in evolution, then the production of that kind of life will also give a sufficient ground for Revelation.

CHAPTER XI

EVOLUTION AND RELIGION

The Christian religion—The Christian goal of life—Fellowship with God—Christian religious ideal realised in Jesus
Christ—Immanence of God—Christ not evolved—Evolution holds for all others—The ghost theory of religion—
Spencer's reconciliation of science and religion—Criticism
—Worship *for* ancestors distinguished from worship *of*
ancestors—Evolved conduct and evolved belief—Universality of religion—Manifestations of religion—Correspondence with reality—Eternal element in religious emotion
—Christianity and evolution—Analogy between evolution
in all spheres and the evolution of Christian life.

IN the life and teaching of Jesus Christ the ethical
ideal is subservient to a further end. With Him
the first and also the last is God. For Him God
is in the world, and everything reveals God. "Behold
the birds of the air, that they sow not, nor reap, nor
gather into barns; and your heavenly Father feedeth
them. . . . Consider the lilies of the field, how they
grow; they toil not, neither do they spin : yet I say
unto you, that even Solomon in all his glory was not
arrayed like one of these." It is God who clothes the
grass of the field with its incomparable beauty. A
Divine power so extensive that nothing can exist
apart from it, a Divine care so minute that not even
a sparrow can fall to the ground without "your

Father," a Divine power from which all other power is derived, and without the exertion of which no power could exist,—such is the vision which Jesus saw ; and which of us shall say that His vision was either wrong or inadequate ? For Jesus, neither the fowls of the heaven, nor the lilies of the field, nor the grass which grows on the mountains, have any being, fitness, or beauty apart from God. They, after their kind, and in their measure, are for God, live and move and have their being in God.

As for man, well men are also for God, and they cannot rest until they find their rest in Him. The questions which men ask, the aims and desires which burden them with anxiety, are of comparative unimportance when looked at in this light. " Be not therefore anxious, saying, What shall we eat ? or, What shall we drink ? or, Wherewithal shall we be clothed ? For after all these things do the Gentiles seek ; for your heavenly Father knoweth that ye have need of these things." Man ought to have one aim, to be filled with one desire, to bend all energies to the attainment of one end. " Seek ye first His kingdom, and His righteousness ; and all these things shall be added unto you."

Thus ethical duties and the ethical ideal of character were insisted on by Him for this further end, that without them men were not fit for the kingdom of God. In truth, this is the burden of the Bible from first to last. From the point of view of revelation the most awful state a man can be in is to be separate from God ; and the greatest terror of the future is to be in separation from God for ever. The greatest blessedness a man can have is to be in fellowship with God ; and the teaching of Christ Jesus in this respect is simply the culmination of all the teaching of Scripture. When we regard His dealing with ethical defects, we find they are looked at by Him and are condemned by Him, not so much because they are ruinous to man and marked in their progress by desolation to society, as because they unfitted men for the kingdom of God, and made fellowship with God impossible. "Blessed are the pure in heart, for they shall see God." And the impure in heart are unblessed mainly in that they shall not see God. Christ Jesus does not set forth moral ideals or enforce moral precepts, as ethical writers do, by a reference to a mere categorical imperative, or to the consequences of immoral action, or to the deteriorating effect of immoral action on character. These are disastrous; but He enforces them mainly because, apart from ethical purity and attainment, man can never see God and never have fellowship with Him. If a man cannot attain to fellowship with God, he is lost, he has missed the aim of this being, he is miserable.

In Christ's teaching, therefore, we have not a God who is absent from His creation, or who interferes now and then with its working, but a present living God, to whom all things owe their becoming and their being, who hath appointed for them the mode and measure of their working, in whom they are; and who is always striving to communicate Himself to them as they are able to receive Him. To the world without life He gives Himself as power and wisdom; to the living world as life, impulse, guidance; to the intelligent world as conscious reason and intelligent self-reference; to the moral world as the source of moral purity; and to the spiritual world as spiritual life. Many hindrances there are on Christ's view to the communication of God to His creation; but the main hindrance is that men are not pure in heart. In order to make men pure in heart, and to make them fit for the communication of God, there have been Divine toil, Divine labour through the ages; there have been the revelation of God, the mission of the Christ, and all the other Divine workings set forth in revelation, on which I cannot now dwell. Thus, if we accept evolution as a method of the Divine working, a working by wise and adequate methods for a foreseen end, revelation itself will be seen to be of a piece with that process of evolution which has for end and purpose the establishment of the kingdom of God. Scripture also is an evolution, growing from small beginnings to greater and greater fulness and clearness until the end. It is impossible, indeed, to place Christ in the midst of a process of evolution; for He claims to be the First and the Last and the Living One; and His exceptional claim will be vindicated by all Christians, and must in a measure be conceded by all men.

But evolution will hold for all others. Even if we grant that the New Testament, the type of life and the form of teaching in it, is the norm for all succeeding ages, it may yet be affirmed that there is still an evolution for all other men. It is now an approach to a standard of life and thought set up

once, and once for all, a revealed ideal which forms
the real standard of attainment at which all men
ought to aim.   In Christ we may see what humanity
ought to be, and what it may become; and through
Christ we may attain the standard and the fulness
of the stature of perfect men in Him.

The Christian view of the world assumes that God
is, and that God may be known.   It is assumed that
there is a kingdom of God, for which all men ought
to be, and for the full realisation of which God is
ever working.   It sets forth the character of that
kingdom, and the means by which men are being
made fit for that end.   But here we are met with
the objection that God cannot be known, and that
we are unable to say whether the ultimate Reality is
personal or impersonal, moral or non-moral, spiritual
or unspiritual, conscious or unconscious; in short,
that we can say nothing further about it than this,
it simply is.   Yet while Mr. Spencer denies all right
to others to say anything about the ultimate Reality,
he allows himself to call it " an infinite and eternal
Energy from which all things proceed."   He speaks
of the Unknowable and its manifestations, and does
not see that if the Unknowable is manifested, so far
as it is manifested it can be known.   It is quite true
that all our knowledge is related to our faculties;
true, also, that being without attributes or powers
of any kind is unknowable : but this does not interfere with the fact that what knowledge our faculties
do give us is objectively real.

It is true, also, that in our process of explanation
we must ultimately be brought down to the in-

explicable. That there is an ultimate principle which we cannot refer to anything more ultimate, we cannot doubt ; but that does not hinder us from knowing the ultimate principle. For example, in physics we cannot get beyond gravitation, and we know nothing of its essential nature ; but we know it as a fact, and we know that it varies inversely as the square of the distance, and that it is constant. We may know the incomprehensible as a fact, and its laws and relations may be a part of the knowledge.

We are not to touch the argumentation of Hamilton and Mansel and Spencer about the absolute, the infinite, the unconditioned. We have no interest in an absolute out of all relation, in an infinite which is the negation of the finite, or in an unconditioned which has no reference to conditions. We leave them all to Mr. Spencer to make of them what he pleases. For the God we seek to know is the God who has revealed and still reveals Himself in the universe, the Author of its being and its glory, the Preserver of its eternal order. The God of infinite purity and holiness we may know, and with this we are content. The living God we may know, and we do not care to think of Him as being out of all relations, or apart from all conditions. But we may think of Him as the Maker of heaven and of earth, and as the source and goal of all creation.

Mr. Spencer and those who follow him, because of these metaphysical puzzles, have denied to religion all objective validity. True he gives us a reconciliation between religion and science. He hands over to science all that is known, and to religion all that

14

is unknown. Religion can begin only where science ends, and must be content with such worship of the Unknowable as is possible in the circumstances. But this would be the death of religion, which cannot live on nescience, nor can it reverence a blank. We see through a glass darkly, yet we see. The vision may be dim and the knowledge imperfect, yet vision and knowledge must be, or religion will perish. In His presence we must feel awe and mystery, and we may be possessed with a sense of what we do not and cannot know. We may find that silence best expresses our adoration, yet there must be a voice which we can trust, or religion, with its emotion, aspiration, hope, will die. In the God we worship and adore there must be mystery and much that we are unable to comprehend, but there must also be manifestation and revelation. God can reach us, and we can find God.

The full significance of the reconciliation proposed by Mr. Spencer was not realised until he published *The Principles of Sociology.* In Part I., "The Data of Sociology," and in Part VI., "Ecclesiastical Institutions," he has let us see what lot and inheritance he will allow to religion. He was bound by the very terms of his reconciliation to refuse to religion any share in knowledge; and he was also bound to regard any attempt of religion to say what the object of its adoration really was as illegitimate. He knew that religion had beliefs, laid claim to knowledge; and he elaborates a theory of religion and its development which makes it an illusion from first to last. Theologians rejected his " reconciliation " before they knew its practical illustration. They will reject it all the more now.

From his point of view he must, he is bound to give to religion an artificial character and an illusive origin. He allows one germ of truth in religion, and only one,—" the truth, namely, that the power which manifests itself in consciousness is but a differently conditioned form of the power which manifests itself beyond consciousness " (" Ecclesiastical Institutions," p. 838); or, as he again expresses it, " the ultimate form of the religious consciousness is the final development of a consciousness which at the outset contained a grain of truth obscured by multitudinous errors " (p. 839). As we toiled through the pages of his *Sociology*, we had not found anything to lead us to suppose that religion had any beneficial purpose whatsoever, or any germ of truth whatsoever; and the sentences quoted above had in them something of a surprise to us. But we saw that on his system it was impossible to assign any function to religion save a recognition of the mystery of things and a vague awe of the Unknowable.

There was the fact, however, that men had been religious always, that they had a belief in unseen powers, or a power on which they felt they de- pended, and that this belief had prompted them to acts of propitiation and worship. How is this universal belief to be explained ? Mr. Spencer does explain it in his own way. His explanation is that " ancestor-worship is the root of every religion." He will not allow that nature-worship is primitive. Idol-worship, fetich-worship, animal-worship, plant-

worship, nature-worship, and the worship of deities
of all kinds are all modifications of ancestor-worship.
The explanations he gives of the process of development are curious, but have not convinced any
impartial student. We do not propose to criticise
them here. We may observe, however, that if there
is such a thing as nature-worship his theory falls
to the ground. There is a striking difference between
his treatment of nature in relation to science and
in relation to religion. "Absolute uniformities in
things have produced absolute uniformities in
thoughts"; and if he allowed nature to have any
relation to religion, he might have to admit that
religion does correspond with reality. Hence the
zeal with which he denies any direct influence of
nature on religion.

The one thing to be explained is, Whence is the
impulse, the universal tendency of man to worship?
There is no tribe without a religion of some sort.
Mr. Spencer gives no explanation of this impulse, no
account of this tendency. Animals have it not; man
universally has. It does not help us much to give
us a hypothetic account of the primitive man, physical, emotional, intellectual, and to trace a supposed
genesis of belief in ghosts through sleep and dreams,
swoon, apoplexy, catalepsy, ecstasy, and so on; for
the thing left unexplained is, How did man come to
have an idea of a ghost at all? And the explanation may be found in the pages of Mr. Spencer,
though he never uses it. "Every voluntary act
yields to the primitive man a proof of a source of
energy within him" ("Eccl. Inst.," p. 838). From

himself he derives his idea of energy, of spiritual life, of continued existence after death. He must have found in himself the sources of the idea of the spiritual, or he would have never thought of it in things outside.

Mr. Spencer's method of dealing with the primitive man is peculiar. "Of the ideas current among men now forming the rudest societies there are most likely some which have descended by tradition from higher states. These have to be discriminated from truly primitive ideas, so that simple induction does not suffice. To the deductive method there are obstacles of another kind equally great. Comprehension of the thoughts generated in the primitive man by converse with the surrounding world can be had only by looking at the surrounding world from his standpoint." But as this is declared by Mr. Spencer to be impossible—"Though we are incapable of reaching the conception by a direct process, we may approach to it by an indirect process. The doctrine of evolution will help us to delineate primitive ideas in some of their leading traits. Having inferred, *a priori*, the characters of those ideas, we shall be, as far as possible, prepared to realise them in imagination, and to discern them as actually existing" (*Principles of Sociology,* vol. i., pp. 96-8)—it is scarcely necessary to make any remark on the logical character of this procedure. The primitive man will, of course, turn out to be the kind of creature required by Mr. Spencer's theory of evolution, and must be also of the kind which will fit in with Mr. Spencer's view of psychology. There are, however, evolutionists and evolutionists, and psychologists and psychologists, and **Mr. Spencer's** view of both is peculiar.

We turn to the **ghost theory** of religion. We have read the extracts in **Mr.** Spencer's *Sociology* descriptive of the beliefs of savage tribes, and similar extracts in other books of the same sort, and we are astonished to find how many of them are not consistent with the conclusion which is drawn. Mr. Spencer says : " The primitive belief implies that the deceased will need not only his weapons and implements, his clothing, ornaments, and other movables, together with his domestic animals ; but also that he will want human companionship and services. The attendance he had before death must be renewed after death " (p. 186). Mr. Spencer refers even to the Roman Catholic practice of masses for the dead as a proof of the ghost theory. Many writers on anthropology constantly refer to the things buried with the dead, will refer even to the ceremonies of military funerals as survivals of ancestor-worship. Is it not obvious, however, that the evidence points in a different direction ? The relation is not one between the ghost and the person who performs the funeral rites ; but the relation is between the ghost and the powers which rule in the unseen world of the dead. The weapons, implements, etc., are given in order to fit the **deceased to deal** suitably with the unseen powers. They are for the use of the ghost, and are not offerings to propitiate the ghost. A large part of the evidence points to this conclusion.

It is not denied that there is propitiation of dead ancestors, but it seems to be secondary, not primary.

The return of the ghost was to be feared if it was insufficiently equipped for the new existence in the under-world. If it were imagined that he had returned, any further offerings might have the double aspect of propitiation of himself—an apology for former neglect and a further and fitting equipment for the other life. It is surprising that this distinction has not occurred to Mr. Spencer, for he had both in existence at the present hour, in masses for the dead and in the worship of saints practised in the Roman Catholic Church. We submit that the larger part of his treatise is vitiated by not having regard to the above distinction. If the view be true that funeral offerings are for the use of the dead, then it follows that ghosts are not thought of as the lords of the unseen world, and Mr. Spencer's theory vanishes.

It is curious, also, how differently evolution acts, say, with regard to ethics and to religion. With Mr. Spencer evolved conduct is good conduct, and the more evolved it is the better it is, until, when conduct becomes completely evolved, it will be perfect. He is careful to show that the development of religion proceeds with due regard and in strict subordination to the process and nature of evolution. But here evolution does not sanction the result. Evolved religious belief is no more true, nay, it may be more untrue, than belief which is not evolved. Why should evolution work out such contrary results? to produce something wholly good in the one case and almost wholly bad in the other case? It all arose, Mr. Spencer testifies, from the fact that religion has not been content with a mere negation, and has not rested in the Unknowable. As religion has never been able to do so in the past, it is not likely that it will cease from striving in the future, to know the Power which it worships, on which it depends, and for which it longs. We àre struck with the fact that, as far as actual experience, observation, and knowledge go, religion is universal; the lower tribes have it as well as the higher.

Religion existed before science, before philosophy, before theology. Even before definite thought was possible to man he was religious, and bowed himself in awe before the unseen and the eternal. And in religion there is always the element of eternity. Man could not believe that death was the end of all; he believed that the dead had some relation to the living, and that both were in some relation to the Power on which both alike depended. The belief in continued existence after death and the belief in the continued relation to the unseen powers are there, however we may interpret them. There is also the unique character of the religious emotions to be considered. There is something common to them all, and the services they prompt have also common elements. When a man bows himself down before what to him is Divine, when he feels the power of religious emotion, he is then most distinctly human. But everywhere this religious emotion is the witness of his consciousness that he is related to superhuman and supernatural beings.

How are we to interpret this consciousness?—as superstition? as illusion? as something which from first to last has no root in reality and no reference to objective truth? That interpretation means that what is deepest in man, that which is earliest and latest, that which is most distinctively human, is also that which has least truth in it. It would mean that all the great emotions that have their root in religion have no adequate cause, that all the great thoughts that have clustered around the names of God and immortality are simply thoughts in the air, that the share which religion has confessedly had in raising man to a higher character and to a noble view of life has been due to a misplaced trust in man's ability to know the Power on which he depends, and the God he seeks to worship and to serve. If, however, this is so, what dependence is to be placed on any human faculty? On Mr. Spencer's terms religion may have to disappear; but when it disappears nothing will remain.

It is true, indeed, that in the history of religions men have seemed to exhaust all possibilities in their search after something which might adequately represent to them the Divine unseen powers. It is true that there is hardly anything which has not been taken for Divine, and pressed into the service of religion. It is scarcely necessary to say anything here of the evolution of religion or to trace its history. It is a large and interesting subject, to which much thought is given at present. To the modern spirit nothing that men have ever believed is indifferent. We have much inquiry into the manifestation of man's beliefs, and of man's ways of manifesting his consciousness of relationship to the unseen powers. Nothing is more wonderful than the elaborate and developed

systems of religion which existed among primitive
men. There are explanations of these elaborate
systems, quite as elaborate as they, to be had in
abundance at the present time. But the perplexity
is, that almost all of these explanations proceed on the
principle that the higher is to be explained by the
lower. It is the assumption that meets us all through.
To explain life by physics and chemistry, to explain
consciousness by accumulation of the unconscious, to
explain reason by instinct, and the higher mental life
of man by the lower life of the brutes, and finally to
explain the higher religion by the lower, has been the
consistent aim and avowed object of the evolutionist
of the type of Mr. Spencer. This much may be
conceded to them, that the higher is after the lower in
point of time.   There was a time in the natural history
of the planet when the higher was not. But what is
last in time may have been first in order of causation ;
for if the higher has somehow come into being, it
must have been involved in being from the beginning.
  Take the idea of religion, then, as manifested in
man, and we find it universally thus, a consciousness
of relation to an unseen power, and this consciousness
has embodied itself in customs, rites, institutions.
We may trace the development of religion along both
lines.   We may trace it in the deepening consciousness of the man, until religion gathers to itself the
whole inner life, emotion, cognition, will, and until
the man becomes through and through religious; or
we may trace the evolution of religions objectively
in the institutions in which subjective religion has
obtained objective expression.   These two factors are

always in inter-relation with one another; each reacts on the other, and a development of the religious consciousness means also a development of religious institutions. Thus the more advanced the man's consciousness of religion became, the more dissatisfied would he become with those customs which at one time gave them adequate expression. On the other hand, the objective factor in religion would have its influence on the development of the religious consciousness. He must affirm that the religious consciousness is in touch with Reality; and the Reality here includes the action of the unseen power or object of worship. Religion assumes the activity of God. Take that conviction from it, and it vanishes. Take from religion the persuasion that there is an ear open to its prayers, and it will cease to speak. But man speaks to the unseen Power, and he believes that he is heard. The religious nature is recognised as a universal fact, and as one which cannot be ignored. The natural assumption in such a case is that the objective reference of this fact would be recognised as real at least until it is disproved. Failing to do this, we have an instinct without an object, an organ without a function, a demand without a supply; and this is the position we are landed in by Mr. Spencer's view.

In all religions, then, there is expressed the idea of the relation of man to God and of God to man, and the relation is real. It may be very imperfectly, or even be very erroneously expressed. Man's conception of God may be very rudimentary, very inadequate, very erroneous; he may think of the

Divine Being as dwelling in an anointed stone, in a lifeless bit of wood, in a plant or in an animal, in sun, or moon, or stars; but as soon as he conceives the Divine Being to dwell in a thing, that thing becomes unique, takes on a new character, becomes for him Divine. He may seek to express his adoration in strange, impure, unholy ways; but he does express it, and not without result. Shall we say that there is nothing real, nothing helpful in this worship? that there is no trace of the Divine in this rude, ill-informed, non-moral mode of worship? Does not Paul say, "Whom therefore ye ignorantly worship, Him declare I unto you"? It was worship, though inadequate, ignorant, wrong. The thing to be insisted on is the capacity for, the need and the practice of, worship. Given these, and there is always the hope that man will learn as he is taught to worship rightly, and adequately.

At the same time it must be acknowledged that there is no subject so intricate, so baffling to our powers of explanation as that of religion. We may trace a line of growth and advance in the evolution of life, in the evolution of the arts and sciences, in the evolution of morals, though there is much here that is perplexing, and there is something like an advance in civilisation generally. But in religion the endeavour to trace anything like progress is scarcely possible. We have no objection to evolution; indeed, would prefer to use it as a method if we could. How can we apply it when we find in all historical religions an ideal of purity and sublimity at the outset and a degraded worship at the close? We have from the anthropologists a scheme of evolution something like this—from animism, to fetichism, to anthropomorphism, polytheism, theism ; yet we have many historical religions in which the process seems to have been reversed, and there is an evolution the contrary way. Religion is the oldest and most characteristic of the qualities of humanity, and yet in religion it is that we find man at his lowest as well as at his highest. Is there something here which has prevented progress, which has made it possible to lose what progress has been made, and which has made the phenomena of degradation in religion which are so apparent to every student of religion ? Is there an element here which baffles calculation, and makes speculation impossible ? Is it possible that, along with an irrepressible desire to worship, there goes also a something which drives a man away from worship ? Is there aversion to God as well as a hungering desire after Him ? Is there a consciousness of two tendencies in human life, one of which urges man to God, and another away from Him ? Is there a competition of two principles in his moral and in his religious life ? It would seem so.

On the one hand a longing to be united with God, and on the other hand a feeling of estrangement and a desire to avoid any approach to Him. What is the explanation of these opposite tendencies ? Here a feeling of persistence, a consciousness of the continuance of the self, and there a yearning after non-existence : how are we to explain these phenomena ? A being in time, who is conscious of transcending time ; a being who needs eternity to realise his own worth, and who is conscious of a moral defect, a religious estrangement from the source of all goodness, which ever baffles his aims at goodness : how are we to explain these things? For these questions are present to man wherever we find him, and they press with the greatest force on those who have made the greatest progress in religious life.

"Gone for ever ! Ever? No; for since our dying race began
Ever, ever, and for ever was the leading light of man.
Those that in barbarian burials killed the slave and slew the wife
Felt within themselves the sacred passion of the second life ;

  ·   ·   ·   ·   ·   ·

Truth for truth and good for good, the Good, the True, the Pure, the Just
Take the charm 'for ever' from them, and they crumble into dust.

  ·   ·   ·   ·   ·   ·

Evolution ever climbing after some ideal good,
And Reversion ever dragging Evolution in the mud."

So Tennyson sung, as he sought to express the changing moods of man and the burden of the mystery of human life. On all hands it will be acknowledged that in ethics and in religion there is a departure from the ideal order of things. Man has not been able to realise his own ideal, either in nature or in religion. In the lowest man or tribe, as in the highest, there is a wide breach between what man knows he ought to be and what he is. How is the chasm to be bridged? We shall get no help here from merely natural processes or merely natural results, for in both we have transcended nature. We are now in a kingdom of freedom, in which persons, with a power of making themselves to be something, have to realise a character; a kingdom not formed by pressure from behind, but beckoned on by a purpose yet to be attained; a kingdom in which man is to use all things in order to realise himself, and to realise himself that he may attain to companionship with God.

Man is in a world of things which ministers to and serves a world of persons; and the world of things has made room for him. It takes up new elements at his bidding, makes new departures at his suggestion. Man, however, finds insuperable difficulties in the way of realising himself. It is not easy to make a world of ethical spirits, or to realise a kingdom of persons ethically and religiously perfect. On the supposition that such a kingdom is a worthy end, that it is worth all the toil of the universe, what might we expect? May we not expect that the Power who has made all will strive to remedy the departure from the ideal order of things, and work such changes as are needed, and as are not contained in the antecedent states of the system? The system is being modified by human action : may it not also be modified by Divine action? Effects may be thus produced which the system in its accustomed movement could not have brought out. Such effects involve no suspension of natural laws, not even a breach of continuity.

Granting to the ultimate Reality such a power as man wields, a power of modifying the world to suit his purpose; grant to God the wish to help and guide man, such a desire as we see in men to help their fellows, and revelation becomes possible and probable.

Rational beings have appeared on the earth, beings with ideals, with motives, with aspirations; who have to realise themselves; and they have missed their way, have made mistakes about themselves, about nature, about God. They have transgressed in all manners of ways. Why should not God be free to help them? why should He not speak to them? and seeing they had formed wrong thoughts of Him, why should He not set them right?

To deny the possibility of this is simply to deny to the ultimate Reality a power which is in daily exercise in the world of men. If we grant the possibility of such a revelation, the question then becomes one of evidence as to whether there has been such a revelation.

Those who believe in revelation think they can give good reasons for thinking so. They point to the character of the revelation. They are able to point to one people, who, not by speculation, not by science, not by being accustomed to a world-wide government, but by some other way, had come to believe in the unity of man, in the unity of the world, and in the unity of God. They believed that in the beginning God made the heavens and the earth; and they believed that man is one. Then, too, they had been able to form a high ideal of man's ethical character and of man's religious destiny. Above all, they had thought of God in a way distinct and peculiar—not only in those characteristics of Him which may be called metaphysical, but they thought of Him as ethical; a God whom the heaven of heavens could not contain, but who could dwell with him who was of a humble and contrite spirit.

They thought of the supreme Creator of the universe, not as One who dwelt far off from the world, who had no interest in the world, no care for man; but as One who cared for His creatures, toiled for them, loved them, who strove to communicate Himself to them, and to make them ever more fit for the reception of Himself. They thought of themselves as sinful, weak, ungrateful, and of God as caring for them and loving them notwithstanding. For them revelation came to mean redemption, and on that view the course of their history is construed by them. The new departures in revelation are conditioned by the desire of God to help man to rectify those departures from the ideal order of things, which man by his mistakes had instituted.

Not suddenly, nor violently was the revelation given, or the redemption made. Slowly and persistently it seems to have grown from more to more, and in accordance with the usual method of Divine working. " By divers portions and in divers manners " God spoke, and in slow progression the process of revelation went on. As the people were able to receive, so He gave here a little and there a little, but in such a way that every part bore the Divine stamp upon it, until at length appeared the full, ethical, spiritual revelation of God manifested in Christ Jesus and by Him. The character of God manifested in Scripture is distinctly a revelation; that is to say, God manifested Himself in another and more personal way, as He could not manifest Himself in nature or in history. At all events, man has not elsewhere reached it. He has always reached

15

something else. Our increasing knowledge of the
history of religion has made this clear, that ethical
monotheism belongs only to three religions, and all
of these are directly and historically connected with
each other.

It is one thing to discover a truth, and another
thing to recognise a truth when it is made known.
And though man could not have, by himself, attained to a knowledge of the true God, he is able
to recognise it as the highest and the best now that
God has manifested Himself to man ; just as man did
not form for himself the true ethical ideal embodied
for him in the life of Christ, but was able to recognise
it as the highest and the best when once that ideal
was made real and manifested to man.

> " And so the Word had breath. and wrought
>   With human hands the creed of creeds
>   In loveliness of perfect deeds
>   More strong than all poetic thought."

The process of revelation was slow, evolutionary,
progressive. Revelation was always related to the
natural, proceeded on it, assumed, rectified it, and
transformed it to a higher character and use. Even
when, as Christians believe, revelation had been
complete and redemption had been in essence realised
in the work of Christ, then began again a slow course
of evolution, proceeding with many a backward curve,
with many a sad reversion, yet on the whole
upwards. This new evolution was with a view to
realise, in man and by man, a standard, actually,
historically, and concretely given in Jesus Christ, in
His character, in His relation to God, and in His

relation to man. It makes no difference to the character of the process of evolution, looked at as a process " ever climbing after some ideal end," whether we consider the end as one already given and known, or as one not yet realised, and so far unknown. The process of evolution of Christian life is a process towards Christ. He is the aim, the goal, the end towards which Christian life in the individual and in society ever tends, and He is also the means without which the end can never be reached.

There is thus a striking analogy between Christian experience and all other experience. Christian experience begins, and it goes on from less to more. It is comparatively simple at the outset ; it proceeds through struggle ; it is hindered by opposition from within and from without ; it wrestles, fights, and conquers. Its ideal rises from day to day, just as its practice becomes more consistent and more uniform. At first it aims at a near ideal—there is some one thing to do, some one bent to subdue ; but soon it finds that to do one thing means to do many things, to subdue one tendency means to control many tendencies. The new aim of life must tend in all directions, and it is found that every thought, every imagination, every feeling, every desire, all our knowledge, all our emotion, all our activity must be controlled, directed, and guided by the new aim implanted in us by Jesus Christ. To work out this new evolution of character, and so to work it out that all opposing forces shall either be absorbed or cast out, is a task of enormous difficulty ; for a Christian soon learns that the new life is inconsistent with all forms of selfishness, of evil, and of sin. This is the peculiarity of the Christian ideal of life. Other ideals are consistent with some form of defect, of self-indulgence, of sin. All love purifies within its range, and casts out what is opposed to it. Patriotism will cast out all that is unpatriotic, and love of family will not permit a man to do anything which he knows to be opposed to love of purity; but these have no relation to that which does not interfere with the sphere of their operation. But the Christian ideal will tolerate no selfishness, no cruelty, no impurity, no defect whatsoever. It is opposed to all forms of moral defect, to all forms of intellectual prejudice and obscurity, to all forms of spiritual perversity. It calls for moral purity, for intellectual insight, and clearness of vision; it demands incessant spiritual purity and progress. The Christian character is bound to grow in breadth and depth, in length, in height, until it attains all moral, intellectual, and spiritual excellence, and removes all defect.

Here there is a new evolution, alike in general outline to all the processes of evolution which have gone before. It assumes all that has been attained in the previous processes; but on the position gained in all the past outcome of the toil of evolution it makes a new departure, and toils upwards towards another and a greater end. He who has this new life is conscious of his dependence, knows that he has experienced a new beginning, and is dependent for progress in this new way on the exercise of some influence in him by the power and energy from which his new life has proceeded. If he is allowed to express his experience in his own way, he will say that by God he has been made a new man in Christ, and his progress in Christian life depends on the grace of God. He feels that apart from Christ he can do nothing, with Christ he can do all things. The growth of Christian character depends on his abiding in Christ.

In this new process of evolution, then, the factors present in all evolution come into clear consciousness, and all the work of God is seen to be on one plan and of a piece. We may learn something of that plan by having recourse to what science has had to tell us in the lower spheres of evolution ; and science might learn something of the factors of evolution by a study of the New Testament and of the facts of Christian life. We might learn from them not to think of the becoming of things as sudden, abrupt, catastrophic, but to think of them as slow, continuous, progressive. But we might also learn not to think of these merely in terms of second causes, apart from the Power by Whom are all things and for Whom are all things. Things are never removed from God, neither in them-selves, nor in their working, nor in their progress. Thus the process of pre-organic evolution will become luminous, for it is working upwards under the guidance of energising Reason to a higher end. They are made to work according to their nature, and not contrary to their nature. Thus there is one kind of evolution in the pre-organic world. When after fit preparation life appears, we have a different kind of evolution, proceeding on different lines, to higher ends. A new element enters in, and purpose rules. All parts of the organism are for the organism, and no part is for itself alone; and the more complex the organism is the greater is the unity of the whole. The inorganic world is in the service of the world of life. One kind of life is also for another; there is not only competition, there is co-operation.

Then there is conscious life, and self-conscious life. And here also there is something new. Here we see the world of things in the service of a world of persons. This is the broad outcome of the cosmic process. Can we say that this is accidental? a mere fortuitous outcome of a process that has proceeded without an aim, or without a purpose? A rational being can hardly think so. At all events, with the advent of a self-conscious being we have a new line of evolution; for the self-conscious being no longer modifies himself organically, he modifies something else.

But with the self-conscious being there appears to be for the time an arrest on progress; for here we come on phases of action which do, indeed, in some instances indicate advance, but also in other examples show the opposite. In moral and in religious conduct there are, broadly speaking, mistakes of all kinds made, and as we saw man was worse than any animal, and more evil than any brute; but he was also higher and better. In truth, he was on a different plane altogether, both in good and in evil. All things are ruled and guided according to their nature: absolute necessity in the pre-organic world, relative necessity in the organic world; but in the intellectual, moral, and spiritual world we have government and

a kind of rule according to the law of freedom.
Thus the new kind of evolution takes on new factors,
and its method must widen itself accordingly. We
may try to translate freedom into necessity, and may
delude ourselves into thinking that we have done so ;
but the fact and the consciousness of freedom remain,
and also the fact of its co-relative responsibility.

The new problem of rational evolution is to persuade
rational beings to be wholly rational, moral beings
to be wholly moral, and religious beings to be wholly
and adequately religious. The Christian view of the
world is the only view which does justice to all the
factors of evolution, and recognises all its complexity.
So much we can see ; but we still see as through a
glass darkly. We see enough to be able to say,
"Of Him, and to Him, and through Him are all
things." But there is much that we cannot yet
understand about the "of" or the origin, much that
is dark also about the process indicated by the word
"through" ; and the goal, though indicated in outline,
is yet only indicated in general terms. While we
therefore humbly bow our heads before the great
mystery, we cannot let go the conviction that there
has been an "of," and there is a "to," as well as a
"through," for the processes of the world. Thankful
are we to all, be they who they may, who can enable
us to see more clearly the process which may be
summarised by the word "through" ; but when they
have shown us all they can of the process, we claim
the right to look at all they discover not as something
which can be in itself and for itself. For it is mean-
ingless unless the "through" is related to an "of"

and a "to," or rather that the facts symbolised by all three words are facts in relation to Him Who in the beginning created the heavens and the earth, Who is the beginning and the middle and the end; by Whom are all things, and for Whom are all things. To all that science teaches us, to all that history proclaims, to all that philosophy in all its branches can teach us, we add the further light which revelation brings, and in that light all falls into harmonious unity. For in Christ "are hid all the treasures of wisdom and of knowledge," Christ, "Who is the image of the invisible God, the first-born of all creation; for in Him were all things created, in the heavens and upon the earth, things visible and things invisible, whether thrones or dominions or principalities or powers; all things have been created through Him, and unto Him; and He is before all things, and in Him all things consist."

For EU product safety concerns, contact us at Calle de José Abascal, 56–1°,
28003 Madrid, Spain or eugpsr@cambridge.org.

www.ingramcontent.com/pod-product-compliance
Ingram Content Group UK Ltd.
Pitfield, Milton Keynes, MK11 3LW, UK
UKHW010339140625
459647UK00010B/692